CRISIS
in the
CHURCH

A Study of Religion in America

CRISIS
in the
CHURCH

A Study of Religion in America

by ANDREW M. GREELEY

THE THOMAS MORE PRESS
Chicago, Illinois

The excerpt from *The Ultimate Values of the American Population* by William C. McCready with Andrew M. Greeley, Sage Library of Social Research, Volume 23, © 1976, pp. 8-10 and 18-19 is reprinted by permission of the publisher, Sage Publications, Inc. (Beverly Hills/London).

ISBN 0–88347–106–X

To Mary and Andy Burd
"Bearers of the Good News"

If there is a God who lives down the street
Scheming and plotting a devious romance,
Starting the music pounding out a beat,
Inviting us, one and all: "Come to my dance!"
If he gets us first by moving our feet
A wild raucous God, grabbing every chance,
Reveling in noise, turning up the heat,
Catching our bodies in a fast moving trance . . .

Swaying at the door, a hand clapping dame,
Fun poking fear, crazy voice making din
Shouting out orders, you're playing his game,
First at the party, dragging the rest in,
You'd make life a long blast, dance all the night
To the madcap rhythms of the Lord of Light.

Contents

Chapter Nine
The Sexuality Issue

Chapter Ten
Conclusion

Chapter One

THE DILEMMA

ORGANIZED religion dangles on a dilemma. The commodities it offers to the world—meaning and community—seem to be immensely popular; but the churches, particularly the mainline denominations, don't seem able to generate much enthusiasm. While the fundamentalist denominations seem to be flourishing[1] and while the charismatic movement attracts thousands of adherents, membership rolls in the traditional, "non-evangelical" Protestant demoninations are declining and church attendance among Roman Catholics has fallen precipitously since the years of the Vatican Council and the birth control encyclical.[2] Many upper middleclass young people are attracted by religion-like communes and various seemingly bizarre religious cults. They find little to appeal to them in the denominations of their parents or in the parish churches of their childhoods. The desperate quest for social relevance which characterized the denominations in the 1960s and early 1970s has not made them in fact relevant to the religious aspirations of their membership. Something clearly needs to be done in the paradoxical situation in which religion is popular and the churches not.

For Roman Catholicism in the United States the problem is especially acute. There have been massive resignations from the priesthood and the religious life, vocations have declined drastically, and the credibility of the church as a teacher of sexual

Crisis in the Church

ethics seems to be eroding rapidly. The leadership of the Catholic Church is caught in a complex bind. On the one hand it must vigorously insist that there is a deep hunger for religion in American society; on the other hand it must insist with equal vigor that it is not responsible for the decline in devotion of American Catholics.

The decline in Catholic religious practice in the United States has been precipitate. In 1963, some 72 percent of American Catholic adults went to mass every week. Eleven years later, at the time of the National Opinion Research Center's (NORC) second Catholic school study, the percentage had declined to 50 percent, down two percentage points a year for the decade. The years since the Catholic school study have been monitored by NORC's General Social Survey (GSS). The two percentage points a year decline continued until 1977, when Catholic church attendance reached 42 percent a week, a decline of 30 percentage points in the space of fifteen years (Table 1.1).

Table 1.1

CATHOLIC WEEKLY CHURCH ATTENDANCE

Year	All	Men	Women	Under 30	30-45	Over 45	Protes- tants (all)
1973	47%	41%	55%	34%	48%	59%	29%
1975	43%	41%	46%	30%	39%	55%	29%
1977	42%	35%	46%	25%	40%	54%	28%

Only a little more than one-third of the Catholic males in the country went to church every week, only one-quarter of the men and women under thirty. More than one-quarter of the Catholics in the country never went to church, including two-fifths of those under thirty, and almost half of the men under thirty went to

10

church only once a year or less. Furthermore, 76 percent of the Catholics in the country would have an abortion, or advise their wives to, if there were a threat to the mother's health; 66 percent would choose an abortion if there were a serious threat of a defective child. (In both respects there was little difference between Catholic and Protestant choice.) Both in devotion and ethical attitudes, then, the crisis in American Catholicism is acute.

The problem of an explanation was epitomized in a richly symbolic vignette at the 1977 Synod of Bishops in Rome. Bishop G. M. Carter of London, Ontario, the president of the Canadian bishops' conference (and in this respect, at any rate, caught in the same complex bind as his American counterparts) summarized at a press conference the work of the synod. Young people, the bishop said, have a strong and powerful longing for religious faith, but there are obstacles to the Church's effective preaching to them—materialism, paganism, secularism, apathy, selfishness, sensuality, the mass media, and atomic energy.* Kenneth Woodward, the religion editor of *Newsweek,* a man deeply concerned about the transmission of religious values to young people, rose on the floor of the conference and suggested that the Church seemed to be blaming everyone but itself for its lack of effectiveness. Given the research findings on the rejection of the Catholic sexual ethic, he said, might there not be something wrong with the Church itself? Might it not be wrong to place the total blame on its people and on the culture in which they live? Bishop Carter responded with the standard episcopal answer when faced with the survey data on the Church's eroding credibility on its sexual teaching: "We don't make moral decisions on the basis of surveys."

------

* Bishop Carter is an enlightened and sensitive church leader. Doubtless the cliches in his press conference statement were hastily put together by a member of his staff. I cite them not to criticize Bishop Carter but as an example of the standard thinking among Catholic leadership on the subject of the obstacles to the Church's effective work.

Crisis in the Church

His answer is an effective one and it terminates conversation, but it is not a response. No reputable social scientist would argue that ethical values are determined by nose-counting. Hence Woodward's question did not suggest that values are to be defined by data collection; rather he was asking whether empirical research might not reveal to Church leaders the uncertainties, the ambiguities, the problems, the needs of ordinary people. Bishop Carter doubtless knew that, but at the Synod of Bishops in 1977, sex was ruled off the agenda. Can one speak about the religious education of young people without talking about sex? No one in Rome during the synod tried to answer that question. Indeed, few people in Rome even dared to raise it.

The problem for Catholic leadership persists. Some bishops myopically deny the problem, but more sophisticated ones are well aware that even their most devout church members no longer accept the Church's sexual teaching. However this may

TABLE 1.2

SEXUAL ATTITUDES AMONG THE PIOUS[a]

(% Disapprove)

| | Chicago | | U.S.A. | |
	Under 30	Over 30	Under 30	Over 30
Premarital sex among engaged	35	84	60	85
Divorce	34	43	44	45
Birth Control	29	29	24	25
Number	(30)[b]	(118)[c]	(26)[d]	(166)[e]

[a] Those who receive communion weekly and pray daily.

[b] Seventeen per cent of all those under 30.

[c] Thirty per cent of all those over 30.

[d] Ten per cent of all those under 30.

[e] Twenty-five per cent of all those over 30.

have come to be and whatever response to it might be appropriate, Catholics are no longer listening to their Church when it speaks about sex.

If one looks merely at the "pious" Catholics, those who receive Communion weekly and pray every day (10 percent of those under 30 in the United States and 25 percent of those over 30), one finds a notable lack of support for the traditional sexual teaching, save among those over 30 on the subject of premarital sex (Table 1.2).

Both in the Archdiocese of Chicago in 1977 and in the United States in 1973, almost three-fifths of the "pious" Catholic respondents over 30 approved of divorce and almost three-quarters approved of birth control. Among those under 30 in the Archdiocese of Chicago,* approximately two-thirds of the "pious" Catholics approved of premarital sex among the engaged and approved divorce and birth control.

Thus the most devout young people in a particularly devout diocese reject the Church's sexual teaching in a ratio of approximately two to one. They may be materialists, pagans, secularists, selfish, pawns of the mass media, as Bishop Carter suggested, but their devotional behavior suggests that they consider themselves dedicated Catholics and are able at the same time to be devout and reject the Church's sexual teaching. Such a finding does not constitute a moral value, but it surely constitutes a datum for serious and self-analytical religious reflections among the Church leadership.

Most bishops would admit this. One prominent bishop said to me in a private conversation, "I can't sleep at night because

---

* The "pious" in the Archdiocese of Chicago are a higher proportion of the population than nationally—17 percent of those under 30, 30 percent of those over 30. The lower level of support for the Church's sexual ethic among the pious under 30 in Chicago when compared to the pious nationally may be the result of the four-years difference between the 1973 national study and the 1977 Chicago study, which suggests an even greater erosion in the half-decade among young people in accepting the Church's traditional sexual morality.

of what that encyclical (the birth control encyclical *Humanae Vitae*) is doing to my diocese." Howeve., such assertions cannot be made in public and are rarely discussed privately.

Caught, then, in the dilemma of strong religious need and declining ecclesiastical enthusiasm, Church leadership has grasped at something which has been labeled "evangelization." Influenced by a recent papal encyclical, impressed by the fervor of the charismatics and by the success of the fundamentalist denominations, Roman Catholicism has recently placed considerable emphasis on "evangelism." Other mainline denominations are also turning to it, insisting that the idea of "preaching the gospel" is very much part of the Protestant heritage. No one is against evangelization. How can one be?

Some "liberals" and social actionists (both Catholic and Protestant) are uneasy about the evangelizing emphasis, fearing that it represents a turning away from social responsibility and a sell-out to the simplicism of "the evangelicals" and the fundamentalists. But you have to do something, and while the impulse to "do something" may be stronger among Catholics than among Protestants because the Catholic crisis now is especially acute, it is a culturewide phenomenon that apparently influences all American religious denominations. (One could go through a litany of explanations: Watergate, Vietnam, etc., etc., etc.)

It is hard to define exactly what "evangelization" means. In its Greek origin, of course, the word refers to the "Good News." Evangelizing means to preach the Good News (although the evangelization emphasis among American denominations does not seem to involve any particularly vigorous attempt to improve the quality of teaching). Definitions either so abstract as to be meaningless or so enthusiastic as not to admit of serious discussion abound. One gathers from articles and conversations that the objects of evangelization are the "unchurched" and "alienated." Having been relatively unsuccessful with their own members, the response of the churches seems to be to pursue enthusiastically those who are not members.

I do not intend to be snide. Preaching the gospel of Jesus is the principal reason for the existence of churches. An evangelization program can be a cop-out, however, a refusal to face the real problems the churches face. It can also be a challenge. Indeed, it is the perennial challenge that all Christians must face. Some of the evangelization emphasis of recent years is responsible and intelligent. Within the Catholic Church, Archbishop Francis Hurley's Ad Hoc Committee on Evangelization does not seem to be running from the dilemmas that Roman Catholicism faces. Still, much of the contemporary evangelization enthusiasm is unaffected by serious and responsible thought. The "unchurched" are out there, and we must go get them! The hard sell is back in fashion.

Doubtless the "unchurched" are there. Some 21 percent of the American population has no denominational affiliation or attends church less than once a year. Fifteen percent of those who were raised Roman Catholics no longer identify with the church in which they were raised, and another quarter attend church once a year or less. If one is to "reclaim the lost sheep" or "proclaim the Good News," then one will not lack a potential audience. Unfortunately, there seems to be little interest among the enthusiastic evangelizers to discover what that audience may be like or what built-in resistances it may have to their efforts.

The purpose of this volume is to study the "unchurched" in America—hence, of course, to study religion in America. Let it be clear at the beginning that this book will bring very little consolation to the evangelization movement as it exists at present.

One has the impression that the enthusiasm is considerable. Many Catholic clergy and religious (and I presume their counterparts in other denominations, too) desperately yearn for "something to do" in a time of uncertainty and lack of clear theoretical orientation. Unfortunately, the "something to do" varies from year to year: sensitivity training, encounter groups, picket lines, "relevance," "salvation history"—the fad changes every year or every couple of years. In 1976, it was "social action" for Roman Catholics—the "Call to Action" meeting by which the American Catholic bureaucracy responded to the bicentennial celebration; now it is evangelization.

Such fads do not affect the rank and file Catholic laity. We will demonstrate in a subsequent chapter that the laity are remarkably immune to bad leadership. But they do affect elite religious functionairies, consuming time, energy, and money. The Call to Action meeting at Detroit in the fall of 1976, for example, had little impact on most Catholic lay folk, since they were scarcely aware of its existence. Two-thirds of those who participated in the meeting were employees of the Church, members of the Church bureaucracy for whom the event was a very important phenomenon. The evangelization campaign, presumably a phenomenon of the same order of importance, will occupy the time and energy and spend the available resources of bureaucratic elites while going unnoticed by the ordinary Catholic and probably by most of the ordinary unchurched. Yet it is not thereby unimportant, for over the long run, the decisions and actions of bureaucratic elites do affect the membership and the direction of large voluntary organizations (which is what the churches in the United States are, of course). No great harm will be done by a shallow, enthusiastic evangelization fad, but what could be lost in one more fashionable outburst is an opportunity to acquire a deeper and more serious understanding of the nature of the churched and the unchurched, belief and unbelief, religion and non-religion in American society.

This volume is an attempt to understand more adequately what religion means in American society. There are five sets of "adversaries" to which the book is addressed.

1. There is a major shift to the right going on, surely in American Catholicism and apparently within the other American mainstream denominations too. The non-intellectual, if not anti-intellectual, enthusiasm of the charismatics, combined with the revulsion against "social relevance" epitomized by the Hartford Statement, engineered by Richard John Neuhaus and Peter Berger, have had considerable impact among denominational elites. Within Catholicism, a number of prominent intellectuals, such as David Burrell, Michael Novak, and Avery Dulles, are now taking a much more cautious and conservative

line than they would have ten years ago. Many other Catholic theologians seem to think that the time has come to draw the line against the trend in theological reflection begun at the second Vatican Council. For those who seek explicitly or implicitly to recall pieties and certainties of the past, the data in this book will serve as a warning that it simply cannot be done. One may well object—and I surely do—to the "watering down" of the Christian tradition to achieve acceptability in the secular academic milieu, but the mindless repetition of the old pieties will not work. The challenge to translate the religious traditions into terminology that is meaningful for the contemporary world remains, even if most such attempts in the past years have been something less than successful.

There is both faith and yearning for faith in the United States, but there is also a profound skepticism about ecclesiastical leadership; and that skepticism includes theologians and teachers, as well as bishops and administrators.

2. My second set of "adversaries" are the enthusiasts, those who think you can short-circuit the difficult, demanding task of rethinking religious heritage and remodeling religious institutions by an ever more vigorous display of intense religious enthusiasm. It is surely the case that religion has not been emotional enough in the past. Furthermore, any effective religion must appeal to the total human personality, emotions included. Unfortunately, as Ronald Knox demonstrated so long ago in his classic *Enthusiasm*,[3] the pendulum swings all too rapidly from hyperrational religion to hyperemotional religion. At the present time we are witnessing a tremendous upsurge in religious emotionalism. Whatever the merits of the charismatic renewal in the Christian church (and my feeling is that they are severely limited), it has done little to develop among American Christians a higher tolerance for complexity or a more sophisticated understanding of the nature of the religious problems of those who are not affiliated with any particular denomination or church. An enthusiastic hard sell, no matter how sincere its motivation or intense its enthusiasm, is not an adequate response to the

Crisis in the Church

dilemmas, the ambiguities, and the uncertainties of contemporary American religion. There is, as the reader of this volume will learn *ad nauseam,* an extraordinarily diverse collection of variables that go into explaining religious behavior. The evangelist who is intolerant of complexity, impatient with diversity, who does not have the time for hard intellectual work, the inclination for patient and careful investigation, will do far more harm than good to the message he wants to preach.

3. The third set of "adversaries" to whom this volume is addressed are those Catholic religious leaders and theologians who think that they can respond to the religious opportunities and challenges, as well as problems and dangers of the day, by pretending that there is no problem with the Church's sexual teaching. The evidence that they are wrong is overwhelming, yet some of them are apparently unpersuaded. Those who bother to read this book will find even more evidence here. Perhaps they will at least be persuaded to look at the origins of their problem, which lie in the traditional sexual ethics developed at a time when marriage was an important economic institution designed to assure the transmission of family property within the family line. One kept alive the efforts of one's ancestors by making sure that their land was passed on to their seed. Premarital and extramarital activity was an insidious threat to that goal. Furthermore, the maintenance of the human race, which meant raising up heirs to one's line and providing oneself with the insurance of children to care for one in old age, required that most women be either pregnant or nursing during most of their adult lives. My colleague Teresa Sullivan has observed that until a century and a half ago in the Western world, 6.48 live births (meaning nine or ten pregnancies, perhaps) were required for a married couple to reproduce itself, that is, to have two children who would live to begin families of their own. The average husband and wife could expect to spend twelve years of married life together before one or the other died. At the present time, ten pregnancies can easily produce ten children who live to adulthood. Most married couples make their contribution to the

maintenance of the human race before they are twenty-five and they can count on 48 years of marriage before death separates them. The profound economic and demographic changes of the last 150 years—little understood by most religious leaders— have totally transformed the ambience of human sexuality. It has therefore become necessary to sort out the perennial wisdom of the traditional sexual ethic from the culture-bound expressions of that wisdom which may no longer be pertinent in our own time. By mindlessly repeating the norms of the past without being aware of the profound change the demographic revolution has created, Catholic leadership has succeeded in discrediting not only the traditional norms but also itself as a teacher of sexual ethics. It has contributed to the deterioration of the under- standing of the perennial wisdom of human relationships of which it is one of the world's oldest trustees. I am neither an ethician nor a philosopher, and I only can grasp dimly the direc- tion in which a reelaboration will proceed. (I suspect the critical word is "intimacy." Data on that subject will be presented in a subsequent chapter.) I hope the evidence gathered together in this book will persuade Catholic leadership that it is not merely materialism, paganism, apathy, selfishness, atomic energy, or the mass media that has caused many of their most devout followers to tune them out whenever they begin to speak on sex.

4. The fourth group of "adversaries" are those who propound the theory of "secularization," the notion that "progress" and "modernity" have produced a new variety of humankind which does not need religion and which is therefore much less religious than its ancestors.[4] There is a peculiar affinity between the enthusiasts and the secularizationists. For if humankind is less religious and if it is impossible to rearticulate the religious tradi- tion in terms contemporary humans find attractive, then, of course, your only response is vigorous emotional enthusiasm; if you can't get the people's intellects, you've got to get their emotions. The word "secularization" has taken on an almost mystical connotation among some theologians and social think- ers, as well as some religious leaders. Such observers are loath,

however, to define the term—almost as though it were a desecration to surrender it for operational verification. When one tries to operationalize their concept and subject it to verification or falsification, they immediately protest that that is not what they are talking about. But they themselves will not define operationally what secularization is, much less do so in such a way that it can be falsified by evidence. An alleged trend in human behavior which cannot be falsified cannot be verified either; it takes on an aura of revelation or myth. Humans are entitled to both revelations and myths, but these should not be confused with objective social investigation. To speak of secularization in a country where more than 95 percent of the people believe in God, more than 70 percent believe in life after death, more than 80 percent pray every week (50 percent pray every day), and 37 percent have had intense religious experiences is utter nonsense. Most secularization theory is merely a projection of the agnosticism of the New York-based mass media and the elite university campus onto the rest of society.* I have yet to encounter a social science colleague who is not utterly astonished to find out that more than 90 percent of the American public prays and half prays every day. Nobody they know, you see, prays all that much, or, if they do, they don't talk about it in the newsroom or the faculty club.

Religion changes like everything else does in a volatile society, and some of the religious changes over the last couple of decades have been dramatic; but "secularization" is not a good name for what has happened. The secularization model is useful neither as social science nor as a guide to religious policy making.

5. Finally, the last set of "adversaries" to whom this book is addressed includes those observers of the American Catholic scene who place most of the blame for the current Catholic

---

* Some such attempts become ludicrous. Three sociologists at the University of Notre Dame, for example, linked the secularization which they alleged (without any evidence) to have occurred among American Catholics during the 1960s to such events as Father Groppi's protest marches.

crisis on the leadership of the Church in the United States. It is a curious experience to find oneself labeled "adversary" in one's own book. Nevertheless, while I yield to no one in my dissatisfaction with the quality of American Catholic leadership, the evidence in this volume suggests that the Catholic crisis and an effective response to it—whether in evangelization or any other technique—have relatively little to do with the quality of episcopal leadership. Inept, oppressive, and insensitive bishops may hurt the Church's public image, demolish morale, and ruin the financial structure of a diocese, but they seem to have little effect on the behavior of the faithful—in the short run, at any rate. It is now as certain as anything can be that the principal cause of Catholic religious decline in the United States is sex—and the highly specific kind of sexual issue represented by the birth control prohibition encyclical. The bishops may be faulted for their sins of omission in attempting to resist the *Humanae Vitae* decision before it was made, but they surely cannot be blamed for the decision. It would doubtless be much better to have more inspiring and more gifted bishops, but the bishops did not bring the American Church to its present crisis, and whether those who have slipped to the fringes of the Church because of the crisis can be brought back by more enlightened bishops pursuing a sensitive and intelligent program of evangelization seems to be on the basis of the evidence presented in this volume highly problematic. The Archbishop of Chicago is unpopular with his people, as we shall demonstrate in a later chapter—as unpopular as Richard Nixon was the year before he resigned from office. Yet Chicago Catholics have been less affected by the crisis in the Church than other Catholics in the rest of the nation. They are both more devout and more generous than the national average and also somewhat less affected by the changes of the past fifteen years. Chicago Catholics seem able to survive relatively unscathed the monumentally inept, and insensitive regime of John Cody: it seems reasonably clear that in the short run, at any rate, as far as the average Catholic is concerned, it doesn't much matter who his bishop is.

Crisis in the Church

Against all these adversaries I intend to make the following arguments:

1. The unchurched are not, by and large, waiting for evangelization. If the field is ripe for harvest, it will still be an extraordinarily difficult and complex task.

2. Much more is required than enthusiastic and short-lived evangelization campaigns.

3. Many of the problems that lead to becoming unchurched (or "disidentified") have their origins in life experiences or influences which are beyond the Church's capacity to affect.

4. The most important and most critical influence in the religious life of Americans is the religion of their spouses. The happier the relationship between spouses, the more powerful and more positive is the religious influence. Given the perceived impact of the Church's sexual teaching on that relationship, the Catholic Church is in a situation of special disadvantage when it tries to deal with the religious needs and problems of the husband-wife unit.

5. There are, nonetheless, many things the Catholic Church (and other denominations) can do to preach the Good News more effectively—most notably, improve sermons, reinforce prayer life, strengthen family intimacy, and respond skillfully to the problems of young people. It is my impression that few "evangelization drives" are concerned with any of these areas where the Church could with some ease improve its strategic position. To anticipate a major finding of this investigation, any evangelization "plan" that does not take as one of its principal goals an improvement in the quality of sermons should be dismissed out of hand as an absurd charade.

The concatenation of three different circumstances led me to think about writing this book. My colleague Professor Norman Nie and his associates at SPSS (Statistical Package for the Social Sciences) developed a "conversational" computer system which made data files instantly available to researchers who use SCSS (SPSS Conversational Statistical System). This dramatic breakthrough in data analysis makes it possible to reanalyze data sets

22

which had become for all practical purposes inaccessible once the original studies for which they had been collected were finished. I spent a good deal of time in the summer of 1977 (too much time, I suspect) scavenging among the unused data files to which I had always wanted to return. Secondly, and at almost the same time, the Ad Hoc Committee on Evangelization, chaired by Archbishop Francis Hurley with Monsignor Richard Malone as staff director, asked me to prepare a paper on the subject of evangelization. It seemed natural to use Professor Nie's program to write one and then several papers for the committee. Finally, the *Chicago Tribune* undertook a study of Roman Catholics in the Archdiocese of Chicago. In return for a consultation about questionnaire design and survey analysis, they made the data from this study available to me for further analysis. I am immensely grateful to Professor Nie, Archbishop Hurley, Monsignor Malone, and Mr. Michael Smith of the *Tribune* for enabling me to think systematically with empirical data on the subject of evangelization. Needless to say, none of them is in any way responsible for the contents of this book.

The Chicago study is especially useful because it enables one to replicate models tested against national data, examine the possibility that there may be geographic or locational diversity in the condition of American Catholicism and to determine what impact the popularity of religious leaders has on the devotion of American Catholics. There has been little empirical research on American dioceses. Only the diocese of Helena has attempted a serious and responsible survey, as far as I know. (I pass over in charitable silence the "quickie" projects such as the much publicized Yorkville study in the Archdiocese of New York.) The *Tribune* data, then, represent the first available body of research evidence on a large American Catholic archdiocese. These data suffer under two severe handicaps: they were collected in a relatively brief questionnaire and from a relatively small sample. The latter problem can be solved by using strict tests of statistical significance (only differences between Chicago and the rest of the country that are significant at the .001 level are accepted). The brief questionnaire is a more serious problem. We would like to know a good deal more about the Archdiocese of Chicago. Still, it must be said that any reader of the Chicago chapter in this book will know more about that city than is known about any other Catholic archdiocese in the country. To those readers who may question how one can generalize about a large Catholic population on the basis of 619 interviews, I would suggest that they either read a text on probability sampling or enroll in a course on the subject.

Chapters 2 to 6 of this book will deal with various kinds of religious dissidence, the assumption being that each form of dissidence represents some kind of opportunity for evangelization. The second section of the book, chapters 7 to 9, will deal with various factors that might have impact on evangelization— leadership, secularization, intimacy.

There are five kinds of religious dissidence which I propose to investigate. They are:

— *Alienation.* Religious affiliation combined with low levels of religious practice.

— *"Unchurchedness."* Either the absence of religious affiliation or a level of religious practice involving less than yearly church attendance.

— *Dissatisfaction.* Religious affiliation combined with disapproval of parochial life.

— *Disidentification.* Leaving the religious denomination in which one was raised.

— *"Communalism" or "voluntarism."* Remaining within a religious denomination but rejecting the authoritativeness of its teaching.

Table 1.3 shows the data sources that are used for each of the chapters, the nature of the sample, the size of the sample, the date the data were collected, and the principal publication in which the questionnaires and methods of data collection are described in greater detail.

A study of evangelization is, as will shortly be clear, in fact a study of religion in America. I have chosen to cast this book in a "policy" rather than an academic format partly because

TABLE 1.3

QUESTIONS AND DATA SOURCES IN THIS VOLUME

Chapter	Question	Main Source	Sample	Size	Date	Publication
2	Who are the alienated?	Catholic school study	national probability	940	1974	Catholic Schools in a Declining Church
3	Who are the "unchurched?"	basic belief study	national block quota	1530	1973	The Ultimate Values of the American Population
4	Who are the dissatisfied?	Catholic school study	national probability	940	1974	Catholic Schools in a Declining Church
5	Who are the disidentifiers?	General Social Survey (GSS)	national probability	9220	1972–1977	
6	Who are the "communal?"	Catholic school study	national probability	940	1974	Catholic Schools in a Declining Church
7	How important is leadership?	Tribune study	local random digit phone (probability)	619	1977	
8	Does secularization explain decline?	basic belief, GSS	block quota, national prob.			
9	What is the role of intimacy?	Catholic school studies, 1963 and 1974	nat. prob. (1974) nat. prob. (1963)	940 2107	1974 1963	(1974) Catholic Schools in a Declining Church, (1963) The Education of Catholic Americans
		alcohol study	phone 4 cities, 5 ethnic groups—parents, adolescent children	980	1977	Alcohol Subcultures among American Ethnic Groups (forthcoming)

Crisis in the Church

I began to think about the subject in response to a request for a policy paper and partly because policy books are likely to be read by more people than academic books. I will confess that unlike many of my colleagues, I care about the general public reading my books—especially this one.

I will pay little attention to most of the published literature on the sociology of religion because I have never found it very helpful. It is especially unhelpful on the present subject. There are, as I see it, five different theoretical approaches in the sociology of religion: the church-sect approach, in which one searches in vain for differential behavior in larger and smaller religious groups; the Marxist or social-class approach, which views religion either as the opiate of the masses or a tool of upper-class oppression; the functionalist approach, which sees religion as a response to the injustices and sufferings of life; the secularization approach, which is so fiercely eager to find traces of the decline in religious devotion; and the Protestant ethic approach, which resolutely searches for evidence that Catholics don't work as hard as Protestants. I reject them all, not on principle, but on the basis of the empirical fact that they account for relatively little of the variance in religious behavior. The socialization approach developed by my colleague William McCready explains substantial and sometimes enormous amounts of the variance in religious behavior (at least by the standards of most sociological models).[5]

One must make two modest assumptions in this socialization approach to religion:

1. Religion is a quest for meaning, an attempt to interpret and to explain the ultimate purpose and meaning of human life. As Clifford Geertz has said, "Man is a creature suspended in webs of meaning which he himself has spun."[6] (Today he would undoubtedly have said "humankind".) Religion is the ultimate meaning system, the ultimate interpretive scheme by which we attempt to respond to the ultimate questions of life.

2. Religious attitudes are learned (not genetically programmed, as Carl Sagan has recently suggested: the Genesis

myth was acquired). We learn our religion; we acquire our patterns of religious behavior from our families, friends, teachers, spouse, and perhaps even our children; we shape our religion as a response to life partly out of the experience of our past and partly in response to present problems, situations, and stimuli in the Church.[7]

Neither of these two assumptions requires us to postulate any mysterious psychoanalytic, genetic, cultural, or economic mechanisms; and they sometimes enable us to explain 20, 30, and even 40 percent of the variance—an extraordinary phenomenon in social analysis.

Many readers will find this a complicated book. I have made no attempt to water down the rigors of its analysis. The reality with which it deals is even more complicated. It is so easy for religious leaders, social theorists, and other wise men to offer simple, sweeping generalizations about the religious behavior of Americans. Their generalizations may be far more palatable and for more intelligible than a twelve-variable model which only accounts for 13 percent of the variance. But at least at the end of my discussion of a twelve-variable model, I can cheerfully say to the reader, "There's a lot more that we don't know." The wise man with his one- or two-variable explanation (secularization, sexual revolution, the mass media, the decline of the family) is in the intellectually absurd position of pretending that he has explained everything. I trust that the modesty of the explanatory powers of the frequently complex models produced in this book will persuade the reader that he should approach the subject of evangelization in the United States with caution, care, and intellectual responsibility.

In addition to those whose help I have already acknowledged, I must express my gratitude to Edward Hamburg and Christian Jacobsen, research assistants, and to Julie Antelman and Virginia Reich for typing the manuscript. My intellectual debt to Bill McCready is acknowledged several times in the book, but his influence pervades it. This teacher, at any rate, continues to be only too willing to learn from his pupil.

Chapter Two

WHO ARE THE ALIENATED?

THE first question to be addressed in this book concerns the "alienated." Why do some members of the Church drift to the fringes without relinquishing their Catholic affiliation? Are these "alienated" Catholics "turned off" by the Church's racial or social teaching? Its failure to support the cause of the "Third World" or of militant feminism vigorously enough? Do they have doctrinal problems? Do they have trouble *believing* the basic propositions of Catholic faith? Is the Church's sexual ethic responsible for their religious indifference? Or is their problem rooted in childhood experiences which have little to do with the stimuli the Church emits today?

It is appropriate to begin by acknowledging both the weaknesses of survey research in general and the weaknesses of the particular data set I intend to analyze.

The good survey researcher is far more aware than most of his critics of the weakness of his craft—the mistakes that can be made, the tenuousness of his assumptions, and the inadequacies of his method. The question may be badly worded or misunderstood; the respondent may answer inaccurately, either deliberately or not; the interviewer may misunderstand what the respondent says; mistakes may be made in coding and data processing; scales may not only be inadequate representations of reality, they may also be inaccurate. The assumptions of the analyst may be wrong.* Also, however precise tables and models of the survey analyst may be, the reality of the world outside is far more untidy, irregular, and unpredictable.

If survey research analysis has so many serious limitations, why use it at all? One response would be to note that the professional survey analyst is more aware of the mistakes of his method of trying to know reality, more willing to systematically take mistakes into account and minimize them, and more willing to express proper qualifications and nuances than are most other social analysts. Precisely because he defines his terms, operationalizes his measures, and lays out his analytic steps, the survey analyst is an easy target for criticism. The armchair analyst, on the other hand, relying as he does on broad definitions, sweeping generalizations, and elegantly simple explanations, is much better protected against criticism, and hence can much more easily make a mistake.

The survey analyst often finds himself questioned about the size of his sample. How can you generalize about Catholic America on the basis of 940 American Catholic respondents? He would reply that normally armchair analysts and even participant observers generalize on the basis of their personal experience and impressions from far fewer respondents and from respondents who are not chosen in such ways as to minimize bias in selection. Since few of us can observe the whole American population or the whole American Catholic population, all of us must use samples for our generalizations. The pertinent question is not sample vs. population but rather size of sample and method of selection. Rarely does the editorial writer, the armchair expert, the participant observer, or the wise man in residence interview 940 people. And rarely is such an analyst

* For the purposes of the present chapter, for example, it is assumed that the dissatisfaction with the Church's racial teaching may be a reason for drifting away from the Church. In fact, as it will be seen in the course of the chapter, there is a positive correlation between support for racial integration and church attendance, leading one to assume, perhaps, the opposite from that presented here.

concerned about possible bias in the selection of those on whom he bases his generalizations.

The survey researcher is willing to acknowledge that there can be mistakes made in generalizations based on a sample of 940 respondents. But because he is committed to careful and systematic work, he chooses his sample according to the mathematical laws of probability in such a way that he can tell you what the chances are that on a given matter the population being studied may be different from the sample being interviewed. He would say, for example, of a given correlation that when one has a correlation of this magnitude from· a sample this size, there is one chance in a thousand that the same correlation will not exist in the general population. (Such is the meaning of "statistical significance.") Not only is he willing to admit that he may be wrong (a trait not characteristic of all social analysts), but he is even willing to try to estimate what the odds in a given case might be that he is wrong.

Survey research, then, does not have the insight of poetry or fiction, much less that of mysticism; it does not have the richness which comes from detailed, sustained psychological observation; it is innocent of the depths of metaphysical analysis and of the high level of explanatory success of many of the physical sciences, but it is still an effective and useful form of knowledge for outlining a broad and general picture of our large population of human beings. It would be an unwise policy maker who tried to base his decisions solely on survey research (as a number of presidents of the United States have discovered to their dismay), but it would also be an unwise policy maker who refused to use the tools of survey research responsibly and to take its findings seriously.

In addition to the general weaknesses of survey research there are some special weaknesses in the analysis being attempted in this chapter. The data set we use was not gathered explicitly for the purpose of facilitating the work of "evangelization." Rather it was assembled to study the effects of Roman Catholic parochial schools, particularly the effects of these schools in the transitional years after the second Vatican Council. A primary research project designed to deal explicitly with evangelization of the alienated would presumably use more precise measures designed for such a purpose. However, since it is unlikely that any primary research will be commissioned on the subject of evangelization, the data set to be analyzed here has the merit of being in existence.

Furthermore, this chapter will be limited to those who describe themselves as Catholic. Nothing will be said in this chapter either about non-Catholics or about those who were born Catholic but who now no longer define themselves as such. (Somewhere between 15 and 20 percent of those who were born Catholics no longer describe themselves as Catholic. For those under 30, that proportion is somewhere between 25 and 30 percent.)

One more preliminary comment is in order before we turn to the body of this chapter: The most successful of the mathematical models used in this analysis explains about two-fifths of the variance. While such an achievement is considered excellent by the standards of social science, it nonetheless leaves three-fifths of the variance unexplained—more than enough room for the operation of divine grace and human freedom. Our analysis is merely intended to suggest that there are certain patterns in the religious behavior of American Catholics. It is not intended to suggest that these patterns are of such a magnitude as to be irresistible. If anything, there is more respect for both freedom and grace in this analysis than in elaborate general public campaigns such as the "Liberty, Justice for All/Call to Action" bicentennial crusade and in any one-variable explanation. (One proposition I heard argued seriously at a public meeting by a Catholic sociologist was that the reason young people are no longer interested in the Church is because of its failure to respond to the demands of the Third World.)

The figure and table below illustrate the kind of analysis we propose. Let us assume a population of students that is ordered on three different scales—their age, the number of years of education they have had, and their scores on the Graduate Record Examination (GRE). Let us assume further that on their ages they may score anywhere from 1 to 25; on education, anywhere from 1 to 16 years; and on GRE score, anywhere from 0 to 100. The correlation coefficient is the measure of the extent to which there is a relationship between one's position on one of these scales and one's position on another scale. Thus the relationship (r)—.32 between age and GRE score (see accompanying table)—is a description of the extent of the relationship of where one is on the age scale and where one is on the GRE score scale. This is a "simple" relationship, and it totally ignores the possibility of any intervening variables.

CORRELATIONS OF GRADUATE RECORD EXAMINATION
SCORE WITH AGE AND EDUCATION

Variable	r	r^2	R	R^2	R^2 Change
Age	.32	.10	.32	.10	.10
Education	.30	.09	.35	.12	.02

Since age is obviously something that is prior to taking the exam, it can be assumed that one's position on the age scale is causally connected to one's exam score. In other words, the older you are, the more likely you are to get a good score. Moving to the next column, r^2 (which is simply r multiplied by itself) is the amount of "variance" on another scale. The r^2 between age and GRE score is .10, which means that about 10 percent of the "variance" on the GRE score scale can be explained by age. Age "causes" 10 percent of the differences among the young people in their GRE scores. But we also note from the table that education relates to GRE score with a correlation of .30, so one's position on the education scale bears some relationship to one's performance on the exam. If age and education were completely independent of one another, their combined influence (R) would be .43 (the square root of the combined coefficients of age and education). They would explain about 19 percent of the variance on the exam score. But a moment's consideration makes it clear that there is a strong relationship between age and education and that a substantial part of their causal influence on exam scores would overlap.

The statistic R is a measure of their joint influence on GRE score, and the statistic R^2 is the measure of the explanatory power of the two variables combined. We see from the table that the R of age and education together (presented in the education row of the table) is .35, and that the R^2 is .12. The overlap between age and education is therefore quite considerable, because when one adds education to the model the R goes up by only 3 points and the R^2 by only 2 points. The final column of the table, R^2 Change, shows the increase in the explanatory power of the model produced by adding education to the causal system containing age and GRE score.

One might assume from looking at the table, then, that age was the principal "cause" of a high score on the GRE, since our addition of education to the model only improves its explanatory power by 2 percentage points. However, another moment's consideration will reveal that this would be a false conclusion. In all likelihood we would realize that what happens is that age is correlated with education and education is correlated in its turn with position on the GRE score scale. Age, then, "causes" the number of years that the young person has attended school, and this "causes" his position on the GRE measure. The relationship between the number of years a person attends school and his score on the GRE may be said to have been "standardized" for the effect of age.

The flow chart in the figure below illustrates this relationship. There is a .90 correlation between age and education, a .30 correlation between education and GRE score, and a .05 relationship between age and GRE score with education taken into account. In other words, most of the influence of age flows through education to the GRE score, which is a "direct" relationship. Older students get better scores mostly because they have had more schooling. The line linking age and GRE score is called the "direct path" between age and exam score, and the lines between age and education and between education and GRE score can be multiplied to produce the "indirect path" of age's influence on exam score. The measure of the indirect path is the product of the two path coefficients, or .9 $\times$ .3 $=$ .27. Thus, of the r of .32 between age and GRE score, .27 is indirect and .05 is direct.

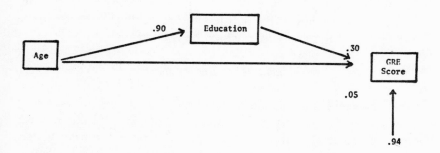

The advantage of the diagram is that it enables us to consider simultaneously the direct and indirect paths by which a prior variable influences a subsequent variable. In this particular instance, for example, we note that even though the addition of education to our model only improves our explanatory power by 2 percentage points, education is the principal channel by which age exercises its influence on GRE score. A small R^2 change, therefore, does not indicate that the variable that causes this rather small addition to the explanatory power of the model is unimportant.

It will be noted that there is a third arrow pointing into GRE score with a .94 at its base. This is called the "residual path." The square of the residual path coefficient indicates the amount of variance in GRE score not explained by the model. Thus a .94 squared is .88. Twelve percent of the variance in GRE score is explained by age and education, 88 percent of the variance remains unexplained by the model. It can be said, therefore, that age and education do in fact play some causal role in a young person's performance on the GRE, but that even when their full causal impact is taken into account, 88 percent of the variance in the position of students on the score scale remains to be explained.

Social science does not expect to be able to explain 100 percent of the variance. Such determinism of human attitudes and behavior can scarcely be expected to exist in reality. The amount of explained variance that satisfies the researcher depends upon the nature of the analysis in which he is engaged.

Variables in the Analysis

The "evangelization" is a proclamation of the Good News. From that proclamation certain invitations follow. In this chapter we are able to deal with six different kinds of invitations which seem legitimate consequences of the evangelization: to identify with the Catholic Church, to participate in Catholic activities, to public devotion, to private devotion, to the practice of charity, and to building up the institution by supporting religious vocations. Obviously, other invitations are also consequences of hearing the Good News, but they do not admit of investigation with the data now available to us.

Table 1 lists the eight variables that are to be the "dependent" variables in our analysis. They form the Catholic behavior which we are endeavoring to explain. The first column names the variable, the second column lists the NORC term which "operationalizes" the variable, and the third column gives the wording of the questionnaire items on which the NORC indicator was based. For the purposes of the present analysis, we will be asking why respondents tend to "identify" with the Catholic Church, engage in Catholic "activities," perform acts of "public devotion" and "private devotion," and express willingness to help the undeserving poor and to support a vocation in the priesthood for their sons.

The decision to focus on positive behavior rather than nega-

TABLE 1

CATHOLIC RELIGIOUS BEHAVIOR VARIABLES

Variable	NORC Indicator	Questionnaire Items
Identification with the Church	Closeness to Church	Indication on a 5-point scale of "closeness to the Church," a "1" representing "the closest possible feelings" and " 5" ..."the most distant feelings."
Public Devotion		
Mass Attendance	Frequency of mass attendance	"How often do you go to mass?"
Communion Reception	Frequency of communion reception	"How often do you receive Holy Communion?"
Private Devotion		
Private Prayer	Frequency of prayer	"How often do you pray privately?"
Visits to Church	Frequency of church visits	"How often do you stop in church to pray?"
Charity	"Help poor"	"Even people who won't work should be helped if they really need it."
Attitude toward Vocations	"Son priest"	"If your son should choose to be a priest, how pleased would you be?"

tive was made solely for reasons of ease of presentation. A correlation between religiousness of one's spouse and one's own church attendance means either that you are very likely to go to church if your spouse is highly religious or that you are unlikely to go to church if your spouse is highly unreligious. The opposite of those variables that are conducive to religious behavior are conducive to unreligious behavior. If you are more likely to go to church because you are pleased with the quality of sermons, then you are less likely to go if you are displeased with their quality. The paper is organized, therefore, around the question of why some people are more religious than others. The reader who is interested in why some people are less religious than others may simply reverse the signs in the correlation coefficients presented in our tables and graphs.

Much of the "religious sociology" done abroad and some of the sociology of religion published in the United States emphasizes "social class" and gender as the principal explanations for differential rates of religious devotion. However, neither of these two factors is very important for American Catholics. This was demonstrated in *Catholic Schools in a Declining Church*. Therefore, I exclude them from consideration in this chapter. (I should note that the models developed in this chapter may operate differentially at different class levels and among men and women, but it is a question beyond the scope of the present effort.) Other possible explanations are summarized in Table 2.

1. *Age.* We know from *Catholic Schools in a Declining Church* that there is a moderately strong correlation between age and religious behavior among American Catholics, a correlation that did not exist ten years ago. Older Catholics are much more likely to be devout and religious than are younger Catholics. Partly this is the result of an influx of a much less religious (in a traditional sense of the word, at any rate) generation under 30, but also it is in part the result of a declining level of religiosity among those who were between 30 and 40 in the early 1970s and between 20 and 30 in the early 1960s. The generation that grew up in the Vietnam years is less institutionally affiliated—

TABLE 2

VARIABLES WHICH MAY INFLUENCE CATHOLIC RELIGIOUS BEHAVIOR

Variable	NORC Indicator	Questionnaire Items
Family Background		
Conflict in family	Family Conflict Scale	Two questions: "When you were growing up, how close were you and your father (mother)? Would you say you were very close..., somewhat close, not very close, or not close at all?" One question: "When you were growing up, how close were your mother and father to each other? Would you say they were very close to each other, somewhat close, not very close or not close at all?"
Family's religious devotion	Family Devotion	Six questions asking father's/mother's religion, frequency of father's/mother's mass attendance and communion reception.
Family's religious style	Family Joy	Two questions: "When you were growing up, how would you describe your father's (mother's) personal approach to religion--was it very joyous, somewhat joyous, not at all joyous, or was he (she) not religious?"
Religious Experiences	"Mystical"	A 5-part question asking,"How often have you had an experience where you felt as though you were very close to a powerful, spiritual force that seemed to lift you out of yourself?"; a list of 16 possible "triggers" of such experiences; an open-ended list of 20 possible descriptions of such experiences; a duration scale from a few minutes to a day or more, and an intensity of the experience scale of 1 (moderate) to 5 (extremely strong).
Religiousness of Spouse	Spouse Religiousness	"How religious is your spouse?" (Very, somewhat, not too much, not at all)

(continued)

39

Table 2 - continued

Variable	NORC Indicator	Questionnaire Items
Religious attitudes		
Doctrinal beliefs	Doctrinal Scale	Three yes/no questions: "There is no definite proof that God exists." "God will punish the evil for all eternity." "God doesn't really care how He is worshipped, as long as He is..."
Sexual beliefs	Sexual Scale	"Two people who are in love do not do anything wrong when they marry, even though one of them has been divorced." "A married couple who feel they have as many children as they want are really not doing anything wrong when they use artificial means to prevent conception." "It is not really wrong for an engaged couple to have some sexual relations before they are married."
Attitudes toward Church as an Institution		
Authoritarian		"Most priests don't expect the laity to be leaders, just followers."
Incompetent	Quality of Sermons	"Do you think the sermons of the priests in your parish, in general, are excellent, good, fair, or poor?"
Social Attitudes		
Racism	Racial Integration Scale	"Blacks shouldn't push themselves where they're not wanted." "There is an obligation to work for the end of racial segregation."
Sexism	Feminism Scale	"It would be a good thing if women were allowed to be ordained as priests." "If your party dominated a woman for president, would you vote for her if she were qualified for the job?"

40

all institutions, not just ecclesiastical—than its predecessors. Whether there is anything special or not about this disaffiliation among young Catholics remains to be seen. Wuthnow[2] sees the change as being something specific to the Vietnam or counter-culture generation and not part either of the life cycle phenomenon of being young or of long-run secularizing tendencies. McCready, Jacobsen and Greeley, in a "Comment" to Wuthnow,[3] suggest that for Catholics under 30 there is less a counter-culture aspect to youthful nonreligiousness and more a "sex/authority" dimension to it. Whatever the explanation, younger Catholics are less religious than their predecessors, and whether the new generation growing up after Vietnam will be any different must await further research, as will the question of whether the Vietnam generation will grow more religious as they grow older.* For the beginning of this volume it is enough to assert that one would certainly expect a positive correlation between age and religiousness.

2. *Socialization.* There is an emerging literature on the relationship between family background and adult religious practice. John Kotre,[4] in his book *On the Border,* and McCready, in his dissertation,[5] have pointed out that family tensions in childhood correlate negatively with religiousness in adult life. Indeed,

---

* There are some traces in the evidence that as the Vietnam generation grows older it grows more religious, though it does not catch up with its predecessors. There is also some evidence to suggest that the post-Vietnam generation will be more religious than the Vietnam generation. (A negative correlation with age is reported in the second section of this report.) There is, then, some reason to suspect that the Vietnam generation is the bottom of a U-shaped curve, that it was preceded and will be succeeded by more religious generations. However, evidence for this conclusion is extremely tenuous. No wise ecclesiastical policy maker would take such a benign outcome for granted.

The American Church seems to be about to embark on a period of enthusiasm for "youth ministry." Characteristically, this enthusiasm is not matched by any serious attempt to understand the religious problems and needs of those under thirty. NORC has proposed a study of Catholics under thirty to no avail—so far.

Crisis in the Church

Kotre found in his study that he could account for almost all the self-definition as in or out of the Church in terms of childhood family experience. The Church, he observed, is an institution that emits many different cues. Which cues one chooses to focus on and how one chooses to interpret them is largely a function of what one brings to one's encounter with the Church. If one brings childhood family tensions, one inclines to interpret the Church negatively.

McCready has elaborated a complex psychoanalytic explanation of God's becoming a surrogate for the father and the family's and Church's becoming a surrogate for the mother. In response to those who seek social class explanations for religious behavior, McCready has also established the fact that the socialization model is far more powerful as a predictor of religious behavior than the social class model. Where you are in the class structure is of less importance than how religious your parents were.

3. *Spouse religiousness*. There seems to have been a decline in the importance of family for Catholic religious devotion since the early 1960s and an increase in the importance of the religiousness of the spouse. This finding has led the authors of *Catholic Schools in a Declining Church* to suggest that in times of stability, it is the family of origin that has major influence on religious devotion, whereas in times of instability and transition it is the family of procreation that has the greater influence. Religiousness of spouse has emerged as the single most important predictor of one's own religious behavior among contemporary Catholics. In this report, then, we will seek not so much to document this assertion as to investigate its implications and ramifications.

4. *"Mystical" experience*. Since William James' *Varieties of Religious Experience* there has been a tradition of thought which has seen a close connection between experiences of the sacred and religious devotion. Greeley and Schoenheer demonstrated in their *Priests in the United States*[6] a relationship between the frequency of religious experiences and a propensity to stay in the

42

priesthood. In a recent report McCready and Greeley[7] have shown a relationship between religious experience and a "hopeful" attitude toward human life. The correlations between "religious" or "mystical" experiences and other aspects of religious devotion have not been high, but they have been persistent in many different studies and justify our expectation that there will be some significant correlation between religious experience and various measures of Catholic identification and devotion. If one has had an experience of the sacred, in other words, one is more likely (though perhaps not much more likely) to engage in the approved and orthodox religious practices.

5. *Sexuality and authority. Catholic Schools in a Declining Church* showed that one could account for all the change in Catholic religious behavior on a number of variables in the decade after the second Vatican Council by the changing attitudes on sexuality and papal authority. It should be noted carefully by readers of this book that accounting for the change in behavior between two points in time is neither logically nor substantively the same exercise as accounting for the behavior itself. It is, for example, one question why Catholics tend to vote Democratic and quite another why the proportion of those who vote Democratic in a given election slides upward or downward. The argument in *Catholic Schools in a Declining Church* was not that sexual attitudes explain why some Catholics go to church and others do not, but rather that changing attitudes (and attitudes toward papal authority) account for the *change* in church attendance. Clearly, then, sexuality and doctrinal positions on the nature of church authority will be *partial* explanations for Catholic religious behavior; but no claim was made in *Catholic Schools in a Declining Church* and no claim will be made here that either factor, or both in combination, is a *total* explanation for levels of Catholic religious involvement.

A word should also be said about the nature of "doctrine" as it is used here. Clearly, the items in the doctrinal index have more to do with religious authority than with the proclamation of God's loving graciousness, which presumably is at the core of

43

the evangelization. The NORC items were originally chosen for the 1963 Catholic schools study; at the time, they seemed unexceptional statements of orthodox Catholic doctrine. Subject to further research, one could at least hazard the guess that they would still be perceived by most Catholics as far more important matters of "faith" than is "loving graciousness."

6. *Institutional Church*. Finally, in the newspaper stories about the East Side Manhattan research done in New York City considerable emphasis was placed on such issues as the rigidity of the institutional Church and the irrelevance to social concerns of many Catholic postures. These stories merely repeated positions that had been taken in the spoken and written word for many years in the more "liberal" Catholic circles. Better sermons, more liberal social attitudes, less clerical domination—these would make the institutional Church far more acceptable to "secular" laity and, in particular, to young laity. While it is difficult to operationalize such pronouncements because they are frequently vague, one might nevertheless legitimately conclude that the assumptions on which the pronouncements were based were that clericalism, bad sermons, and weak stands on sexism and racism were reasons why many if not most Catholics were lax in their religious practice.

By way of summary, age, family background, religious experience, spouse's religiousness, attitudes on doctrine and sexuality, social attitudes, and attitudes toward the institutional Church have all been advanced as reasons to explain why some Catholics go to church and others do not—and, at least implicitly, as strategies to be pursued in any attempts at "evangelizing" among American Catholics. The intention of this report is not to choose among these explanations but to examine their relative importance. Obviously, no single reason can account for religious devotion. The most plausible explanation would be one that takes into account *all* of the factors described in the previous paragraphs.

Analysis

Our third table not unsurprisingly justifies a multivariate approach. Of the 108 cells created by examining the relationships between our independent and dependent "religious behavior" variables, only eleven are not statistically significant. All of the explanations described in the previous section turn out to be valid except one: racial integration. The more sympathetic one is to racial integration, the more likely one is to be religiously active and devout.

Among the other variables, age, family background, doctrinal and sexual attitudes, and sermons seem to be the strongest predictors, with clericalism and feminism (the "liberal" explanation) generally being somewhat weaker. Impact of spouse's religiousness is especially strong at the left-hand of the table (closeness to the Church, Catholicity, frequency of mass attendance [Freqmass] and frequency of communion [Freqcomm]), while personal religious experience made its greatest effect on private prayer, support for a priestly vocation for one's son, and willingness to help the undeserving poor. Age also seems to be a somewhat weaker predictor on the right-hand side of the table when compared to the left-hand side, though taking into account the generally lower numbers of the correlation coefficients dealing with private devotion, supporting the poor and the priesthood, age is still not an unimportant factor in explaining even these attitudes.

When all significant relationships with a given dependent variable are combined into one explanatory model, 37 percent of the variance on the closeness to the Church item, 40 percent of the Catholicity scale, 27 percent of the variance in the frequency of mass attendance, and 30 percent of the variance in the reception of communion can be accounted for—a relatively high level of explanatory power for most social science research (Table 4). A multivariate approach is fairly successful. One can account for somewhere between one-fourth and two-fifths of the variance in self-definition, activity, and public devotion among Roman

TABLE 3

CORRELATIONS WITH CATHOLIC RELIGIOUS BEHAVIOR

Variable	Closeness	Catholicity	Frequency Mass	Frequency Communion	Frequency Pray	Frequency church visits	Help Poor	Son Priest
Age (older)	.34	.31	.19	.23	.16	.17	.12	.09
Family Background								
Conflict (low)	.30	.22	.16	.13	.12	.14	.08	.09
Devotion (high)	.14	.30	.24	.26	.06	.12	.12	.09
Joy (high)	.27	.28	.22	.22	.19	.17	.16	.09
Religious Experiences	---*	---	.10	.12	.16	.13	.12	.15
Spouse's Religiousness	.36	.36	.32	.34	.06	---	.14	.12
Religious Attitudes								
Doctrinal (orthodox)	.26	.37	.26	.29	.26	.24	.10	.17
Sexual (orthodox)	.40	.44	.34	.38	.19	.25	.17	.25
Attitudes toward Institution								
Clericalism (no)	---	.12	.20	.19	---	.07	---	.12
Sermons (good)	.35	.32	.26	.26	.18	.19	.16	.16
Social Attitudes								
Racial Integration (pro)	---	.11	.10	.12	.08	---	.15	.18
Feminism (pro)	---	-.12	-.20	-.19	-.17	-.18	---	---
Proportion of the variance explained by combining all "significant" variables.	.37	.40	.27	.30	.18	.11	.07	.14

*Only statistically "significant" correlations are given. This means that the chances are 1 in a thousand or less that the cor-
relation observed in the sample does not exist in the real population.

Catholics by using the predictor (independent) variables listed in Table 2. Catholics are more religious, in other words, because of such things as age, family background, religious experience, spouse's religiousness, religious attitudes, attitudes toward ecclesiastical institutions, and social and political attitudes.

TABLE 4

PROPORTION OF EXPLAINED VARIANCE*
(Per Cent)

Variable	Varience Explained	Proportion of Explanation Attributable to "Current" Attitudes
Catholicity	33	33
Closeness	27	30
Frequency Mass	20	30
Frequency Communion	20	20
Frequency Pray	12	44
Frequency Visit	11	45
Help Poor	05	00
Son Priest	05	20

But there are two obvious questions. First of all, what is the relevant impact of the past and the present on the religious behavior of Catholics? Some of the variables—age, family background, religious experience (which apparently begins in the late teen years), and the choice of one's spouse—are all things that happened in the past and hence, presumably, are beyond the control of any attempts of evangelization. Other variables—doctrinal and sexual beliefs, clericalism, sermons, feminism—represent attitudes which respondents have at the present time and which may be subject to change, depending upon the influences that are brought to bear on such attitudes. How much of the problem, in other words, deals with the past and how much with the present?*

A second question is whether one can determine which are the most important of the "current" attitudes for affecting religious behavior after we hold constant such things out of the past as age, family of origin, religious experience, and family of procreation. Given the impact of background, in other words, is sexuality, doctrine, sermons, feminism, or clericalism the most important explanation for religious involvement? Or are we once again dealing with a multivariate model in which each of these attitudes seems to play an unimportant role by itself?

The remainder of the analysis is devoted to an attempt to answer these two questions.

The mathematical, diagrammatic and logical assumptions of path analysis (as well as the limitations of human capacity to comprehend more than a small number of boxes and lines) require that a number of variables be combined in order to elaborate a causal model such as that contained in Figure 1. The three family variables are combined into a "family" index, and the five current attitudes are combined in a "current attitude" index. Some of the explanatory power of a model is affected by such

---

* The question of the mutual effect of spouse's religiousness on one's own religiousness is complex, since, as we shall see, there is virtually no relationship between the religiousness of one's family of origin and the religiousness of one's spouse. There is at least the possibility that the married couple together works out a subtle mutual arrangement relatively independent of family background on the matter of religion. McCready reports that in a 1963 NORC study, it would appear that wives had more influence than husbands in such matters when the religiousness of both families is the same. However, since 1963, the importance of family of origin has gone down and the family of procreation has risen in importance as a predictor of respondent's religiousness. Much more elaborate data than those presently available will be required to answer these kinds of questions satisfactorily. For the present report, we assume in our model that spouse's religiousness is a "background" variable, at the same time realizing that the issue is considerably more complicated than that.

combinations, but the goal is not so much to preserve explanatory power as to sort out the relative importance of various phases of the model.

The assumptions in the theory modeled in Figure 1 are as follows:

1. Age (or family of birth) will affect the religiousness of the family of origin.

2. Both age and the religiousness of one's family will in turn affect the quantity of religious experiences one has.

3. Age, family of origin, and religious experience will affect family of procreation (the religiousness of one's spouse).

4. All of these three variables (which may be combined under the rubric "background") will in their turn influence current attitudes.

5. Finally, religious attitudes and behavior will be influenced by all of the five prior variables.

If the predictions made in the preceding hypotheses are sustained by the data, a line can be drawn from the prior variable to the consequent variable; if there is not a statistically significant correlation, no line is drawn. One can see in Figure 2, for example, that religious experience drops out of the model entirely when Catholicity is a dependent variable. The religiousness of one's family of origin does not influence the religiousness of one's spouse or one's current attitude; neither does the religiousness of one's spouse influence one's current attitude. Age, on the other hand, directly influences all four of the subsequent variables, and the three remaining intervening variables—spouse, family, and current attitudes—also directly influence Catholicity.

The "complete" Model B is verified by four indicators of Catholic practice—closeness to Church, Catholicity, the frequency of mass attendance, and the frequency of communion reception. The betas (standardized coefficients—that is to say, coefficients that take into account the mutual relationships of one coefficient to the other, what might be termed the "pure" effect) are shown for each dependent variable. (The column "Freqpray" is presented in Figure 2 to facilitate later comparison with Figure 5.)

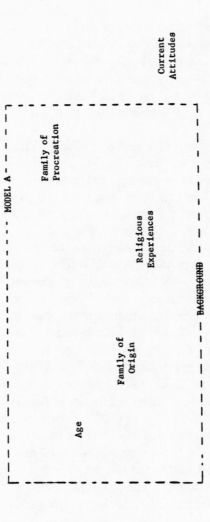

Figure 1—A Theory to Explain Religious Behavior of Catholics in the United States.

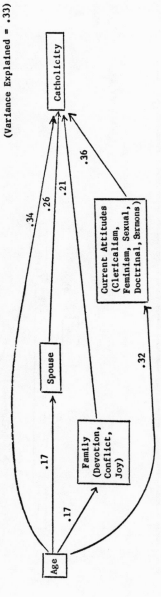

Figure 2--"Religious Behavior Model B." Complete Models.

(Variance Explained = .33)

Current Attitudes
(Clericalism,
Feminism, Sexual,
Doctrinal, Sermons)

Family
(Devotion,
Conflict,
Joy)

"Betas" (Standardized Coefficients) for Other Three Complete Models

	Closeness	Freqmass	Freqcomm	Freqpray
Age	.32	.19	.20	.07
Family	.19	.17	.17	.20
Spouse	.24	.26	.29	.04
Current	.31	.27	.22	.25
(Variance Explained)	.27	.20	.20	.12

51

Figure 3--Four Incomplete Versions of Model B.

I.

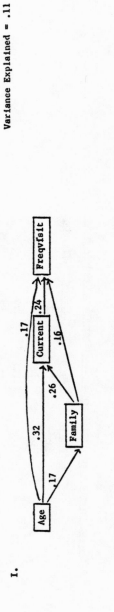

Variance Explained = .11

II.

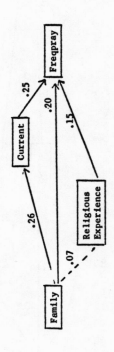

Variance Explained = .12

52

Figure 3 continued.

III.

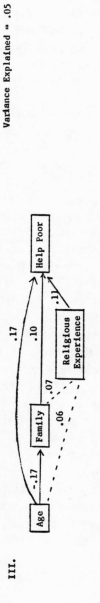

Variance Explained = .05

IV.

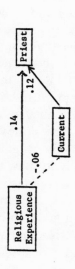

Variance Explained = .05

53

Crisis in the Church

Age and current attitudes are the strongest predictors, and family of procreation is stronger than family of origin as a predictor. Current attitudes, in other words, are an important determinant of religious practice and devotion, but the three "background" factors are also individually very important, leading one to suspect that much of the problem of evangelization—at least as discussed here—arises from situations strongly influenced by the past.

In Figure 3, we turn to four "incomplete" versions of Model B, all of which explain substantially less variance than do the four complete models. Spouse's religiousness has no impact on frequency of visits to church to pray; age.and spouse have no significant impact on the frequency of private prayer, but one's own personal religious experience does. One's attitude toward helping the undeserving poor is independent both of spouse's religiousness and current attitudes. (So much for the relationship between "relevance" and charity!) But religious experience does have a moderate though significant relationship to benign attitudes toward the undeserving poor. Religious experience and current attitudes combine to explain a very modest 5 percent of the variance in one's attitude toward a priestly vocation for one's son. The dotted lines in the incomplete models represent statistically insignificant correlations that are put in the figure merely to show the calculations were done.

It is interesting to note that there is no significant relationship between age and religious experience. The sense of being in direct and immediate contact with the ultimate forces of the universe, in other words, is randomly distributed in the population without regard to age. Young people are as likely to have it as old people and vice versa. (Though, as we will see in the second part of this chapter, religious experience is a more important predictor of other kinds of religious behavior for young people than it is for adults—a point certainly worth pursuing further if research is ever to be done on the religious problems of young people.)

Having established the utility of the causal model for describing dynamics of religious behavior among American Catholics, we can now address ourselves to the first of the two guiding questions of this analysis: How important are current variables relative to background variables? How do we sort out the influence of current variables?

The answer to the first question is that current variables are not, relatively speaking, all that important. The first column in Table 4 lists the proportion of the variance that can be accounted for by our truncated multivariate Model B. If all human behavior could be explained by the model, the correlation would be 1.0. Our predictor variables enable us to explain about a third of the variance in Catholicity, about a quarter of the variance in closeness to the Church, and about a fifth of the variance of mass attendance and communion reception (and lesser influence and variance in the other four). By the cautious standards of social science when applied to such complex matters as religious behavior, such explanatory power can be considered a sign of moderately successful model construction.

However, within the explanatory power the preponderance of the weight in each case must be given to background factors. Thus, if one looks down the second column in Table 4, one sees that only one-third of the variance explained in Catholicity is attributable to current attitudes (or about .11 of the variance); and a little less than one-third of the total variance explained in closeness and mass attendance can be accounted for by current attitudes. Only a fifth of the variance in the reception of communion is attributable to current attitudes. To put the matter differently, 67 percent of the success of our model with Catholicity, 70 percent of its success with closeness to Church and mass attendance, and 80 percent of its success in explaining frequency of communion must be credited to background factors. (We should note that current attitudes are a more important proportion of the explained variance for private devotion—but then, not much of the variance in private devotion is explained by our model.)

The first melancholy conclusion for those who embark on

Crisis in the Church

evangelization must be that insofar as our social science data is able to illumine the problem of religious behavior (or, more specifically, the problem of nonreligious behavior), it locates most of the problem in the past experience of adults. Religion, then, is a profound phenomenon not merely because it wrestles with the ultimate questions but also because it is rooted in the depths of human personality and the past experience of that personality.

One may grant that much of the explanation for people's religiousness is that it is rooted in their past, but the question remains as to how to sort out the influence of current variables. Our Model C in Figure 4 assays an answer to that question. All the background presented in the figure—family, spouse, age, and religious experience—are combined into one "super" background variable. The current attitude composite is broken back down into its component parts. Coefficients between background and the individual components of "current" shows the intensity of the effect that background has on present attitudes. It has a very strong effect on sexual attitudes and attitudes toward sermons, a less strong effect on the other three variables.

Of the five "current" factors, "doctrine" has the strongest relationship with closeness, mass, communion, and prayer. The importance of sexual attitudes declines appreciably. The reason for this is that the correlation between sex and background (.46) is much higher than the correlation between background and doctrine (.13). One's sexual attitudes, in other words, are far more important as a channel for the influence of the background factors than are one's doctrinal attitudes. In terms of evangelization, one might argue that there is some increment in advantage in dealing with doctrine, because that is less influenced by background and hence presumably more amenable to contemporary influence than is "sex." On the other hand, one's sexual attitudes do indeed have an influence on everything but the frequency of private prayer (which is influenced only by doctrine and sermons). Those attitudes must be taken seriously in any attempt to deal with the reality of current attitudes that affect religious practice and involvement.

Figure 4--Relative Importance of "Current" Variables when "Background" is Taken Into Account ("Model C").

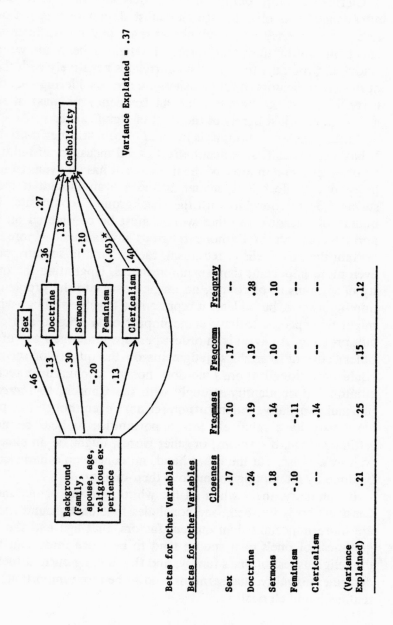

Variance Explained = .37

Betas for Other Variables

	Closeness	Freqmass	Freqcomm	Freqpray
Sex	.17	.10	.17	--
Doctrine	.24	.19	.19	.28
Sermons	.18	.14	.10	.10
Feminism	-.10	-.11	--	--
Clericalism	--	.14	--	--
(Variance Explained)	.21	.25	.15	.12

Crisis in the Church

Clericalism drops out of all the models save the one for mass attendance. This objection to clericalist domination seems only to affect frequency of attendance at mass and not to have any effect on any of the other forms of religious behavior we are studying. Sympathy for feminism correlates negatively with three of the five indicators of religiousness we are considering—Catholicity, closeness to the Church, and frequency of mass attendance—though just barely at the level of significance.

Attitudes toward sermons is in some sense a "sleeper" variable. It has a statistically significant effect on all measures of religious involvement, and in three of the five cases it has an even stronger independent effect than sexual attitudes even though it has a strong (.3) relationship with the "background" composite. The quality of sermons, in other words, must be considered an important correlate of Catholic religious involvement—more important than clericalism, feminism, racism, and in some respects even more important than sexual attitudes. Upgrading the quality of sermons is, of course, no magic answer to the problem of unreligiousness, but at least it represents a feasible strategy which might be expected to have some impact on a tangled and difficult problem. A caveat is in order: perhaps more than any of the other "current" variables, judgments on the quality of sermons could be rationalization. One does not go to church or receive communion or identify strongly with the Church, so *therefore* one makes negative judgments on sermons even though one presently may have relatively few opportunities to hear sermons. Attitudes toward sermons, in other words, might be an effect as well as a cause. On the other hand, no conceivable harm could be done by attempting to improve their quality.

In summary, then, when all the whittling away of our model construction is finished, one concludes that background factors are more important than current factors, that age and the religiousness of one's own spouse tend to be more important than the religiousness of one's family, and that among current factors, doctrine, sexuality, and sermons tend to be more important than feminism and clericalism.

The Young

Since there is a powerful correlation between age and religious behavior, that is, the more youthful one is the less likely one is to be religious, it seems appropriate to discuss the evangelization of the young. If we turn for a moment from correlation coefficients to percentages (Table 5), we see dramatic evidence of how acute the need for evangelization is among Catholics who are thirty and younger. A little better than one-third of them go to weekly church, two-fifths go to church less than once a month, only 13 percent receive communion every week, half receive communion once a year or less, almost three-fourths approve of premarital sex among the engaged, more than four-fifths approve remarriage after divorce, more than nine-tenths approve of artificial birth control, more than half reject the Church's right to teach what one should believe about abortion, only a fifth are committed to papal infallibility, and only a third to the primacy of the pope as successor to Peter. They are half as likely (12 percent) to think the sermons in the parish are excellent, though there is no statistically significant difference between them and those over thirty in their judgment that priests expect the laity to be followers. Two-fifths (as opposed to one-fourth of those over thirty) supported the ordination of women in 1974. (Recent Gallup surveys indicate a dramatic upswing in support of the ordination of women—in all likelihood a backlash to the Roman statement on the subject.) It would now appear that over half of those under 30 support the ordination of women.

The problem of evangelizing the young appears to be even more acute when one pauses to reflect that approximately one-quarter of those under thirty who were baptized Catholics would no longer define themselves as Catholic. Thus one has to conclude that a very substantial majority of baptized Catholics under thirty are no longer Catholic in any traditional sense of the word. Either they have left the Church completely or they reject most traditional Catholic propositions and practices. One would be tempted to say that the task of evangelizing such a clearly un-

Crisis in the Church

TABLE 5

RELIGIOUS BEHAVIOR AND ATTITUDES OF CATHOLICS
(Per Cent)

Attitudes and Behavior	Over 30 (n=646)	Under 30 (n=270)
Weekly church	57	37
Church less than once a month	30	40
Communion weekly	31	13
Communion once a year or less	39	49
Prayer once a day	63	52
Prayer at least once a week	83	81[*]
Very pleased with a son choosing the priesthood	53	43
Sermons are excellent	25	12
Priest expect laity to be followers	44	41[*]
Approve premarital sex among engaged couples	30	73
Approve remarriage after divorce	70	82
Approve birth control	76	92
Church has the right to teach what Catholics should believe about abortion	58	45
Pope is infallible when he speaks as the head of the church (certainly true)	37	22
Support ordination of women	25	39
Pope is head of church as successor to Peter (certainly true)	45	34

[*]Difference not statistically significant.

religious generation is virtually an impossible one, and yet more than half of the Catholics under thirty say they pray more than once a day, and four-fifths of them pray at least once a·week (a proportion not statistically different from the 83 percent over thirty who pray that often). If one prays daily or at least weekly, one must obviously be convinced that there is a legitimate object of one's prayer and some reasonable grounds for addressing that object in prayer. The generation under thirty may well have turned against the Church in substantial proportions, but it does not seem to have turned against God or religion.

I propose in the remaining paragraphs of this chapter to apply to those under thirty the same models applied to those over thirty to see whether the dynamics of youthful religiousness (and unreligiousness) are different from those at work in the general Catholic population. It is clear that the task of evangelization is much greater in terms of sheer numbers among the young than it is among those over thirty, but is there a different causal system at work? Is it merely more of the same kind of problem among the young or a qualitatively different one?

The NORC racism scale was dropped from the analysis of the general population because it correlates positively rather than negatively with religious behavior. It might be argued, however, that young people might react differently than older people because they take their political and social responsibilities more seriously. There might, in fact, be a reversal of the correlation among those under thirty. However, if anything, the opposite is the case (Table 6). Using both NORC's school integration scale and general integration scale, the only significant correlations between racial attitudes and religious behavior are positive. The

TABLE 6

CORRELATIONS BETWEEN TWO RACIAL SCALES AND RELIGIOUS
BEHAVIOR FOR CATHOLICS UNDER 30

Behavior	General Integration Scale (Pro-integration	School Integration Scale
Catholicity	--	--
Closeness to Church	.16	.--
Frequency Mass	.10	--
Frequency Communion	.10	.18
Frequency Pray	--	.14

61

Crisis in the Church

more prointegrationist you are the more religious you are likely to be (or, as seems more probable, vice versa). There is no consolation for those who demand relevance on ·race within the Church to reclaim the sheep that have strayed from the fold.

As might be expected among the young, age is less important than it is among the general population, the age span running only from 18 to 30 (Figure 5). There is only one significant correlation between age and religiousness, a *minus* .13 correlation between age and the Catholicity variable. Among those between 18 and 30, it is the *younger* who are more likely to score high on this composite measure of Catholic affiliation, suggesting perhaps that the post-Vietnam young people are less "turned off" by the ecclesiastical institutions than their immediate predecessors. Furthermore, in Figure 5, there are also negative correlations between age and religiousness of spouse, and age and the report of religiousness in the family, suggesting again a possible revival among the very young. Finally, there is a positive relationship for young people between religious experience and current attitudes and between religious experience and Catholicity, as well as prayer, hinting that religious experience, while no more frequent among the young than among those over thirty, may play a somewhat more important role in their religious lives—thus raising the possibility that the committee might want to consider whether the very considerable interest among those under thirty in such phenomena as transcendental meditation and yoga would suggest that the evangelization of the young should assume a revitalization of the Catholic mystical tradition, a tradition which is, to say the least, dormant in the American Church.

If one compares the beta coefficients in the lower left-hand corner of Figure 5 with those in the lower left-hand corner of Figure 2, one can see that often they are virtually the same. If anything, the religiousness of one's families of origin and procreation (if one is married) are even more important for the young than they are for the rest of the Catholic population. More important for our present purposes, however, is the fact that

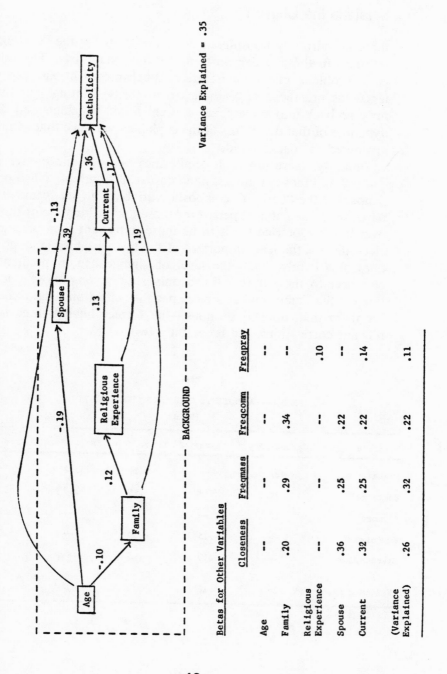

Figure 5--Model B Applied to Catholics Under 30.

Variance Explained = .35

Betas for Other Variables

	Closeness	Freqmass	Freqcomm	Freqpray
Age	--	--	--	--
Family	.20	.29	.34	--
Religious Experience	--	--	--	.10
Spouse	.36	.25	.22	--
Current	.32	.25	.22	.14
(Variance Explained)	.26	.32	.22	.11

there are virtually no differences in the betas for the "current" attitudes in those under thirty and those over thirty. The religious problems of the young are as much rooted in past experiences as are those of Catholics over thirty, hinting that one must go back into adolescence and childhood to understand the dynamics of that two-thirds of the explained variance that can be attributed to "background."

Similarly, there are basic similarities between the figures in Table 7 and those in the left-hand corner of Figure 4. When one "unpacks" the "current" composite variable into its constituent parts, the same patterns persist for those under thirty as for those over thirty. Doctrine tends to be more important than sex, and clericalism is the least important of the five variables (though it does also barely reach the level of significance in predicting closeness to the Church). The only shift among those under thirty is that feminism has a more negative effect on religiousness for them than do bad sermons—the former having three significant correlations, the latter only two.

TABLE 7

MODEL C APPLIED TO CATHOLICS UNDER 30

(Betas)

Variable	Catholicity	Closeness	Freq. Mass	Freq. Comm.	Freq. Pray
Sexual	.37	--	.19	.14	--
Doctrinal	.29	.25	.25	.17	.25
Sermons	.12	--	--	--	.14
Feminism	--	-.15	-.20	--	-.15
Clericalism	--	.10	.15	--	--
(Variance Explained	.26	.18	.30	.02	.11

One concludes, then, that while the magnitude of the problem of evangelizing the young is greater, there are no major differences in the causal pattern at work. The background variables are more important than the current variables, and doctrine and sexuality are more important than the social and institutional variables. Religious experience plays a more central role for young people than it does for those over 30, and feminism and clericalism rise somewhat in importance while sermons decline somewhat—possibly because so few of the young people even hear sermons anymore.

The Chicago Alienated

As we shall see in a subsequent chapter, Catholics in Chicago are more devout and less affected by the changes in the Church than Catholics in the nation as a whole. Thus, as far as the United States is concerned, "urbanization"—so dearly beloved by the European "religious sociologists"—does not seem to be an important factor in leading to alienation from the Church. But the question remains as to whether different dynamics operate in a big-city milieu to affect religious behavior. Chicago Catholics are much better educated than the national average (40 percent of them have attended college); does this fact mean that they are more turned off by bad sermons than Catholics in other parts of the country? Are they more likely to be affected by clerical leadership? Are they even more likely than less sophisticated Catholics to be alienated by the Church's sexual ethic?

If one compares Table 8 with Table 3, one can see that there is a fundamental similarity between the correlates of religious devotion (or religious alienation) in Chicago and nationally. Both clericalism and sermons seem to have a somewhat lower influence in Chicago than in the nation, and the religiousness of one's spouse is even more important in predicting the mass attendance and communion reception of a respondent in Chicago than it is in the rest of the country. It may well be that in a sophisticated cosmopolitan urban environment husband and wife

TABLE 8

ALIENATION IN CHICAGO

	Closeness to Church	Mass	Communion	Prayer	Son a Priest
Age	.22	.19	.09	.23	*
Parental religiousness	.09	.19	.19	.11	*
Spouse's religiousness	.25	.57	.47	.05	.17
Doctrinal attitudes	.23	.29	.28	.16	.13
Sexual attitudes	.28	.32	.35	*	.14
Clericalism (no)	*	.11	.13	.09	.22
Sermons (good)	.24	.21	.15	.16	.13
Racial integration (pro)	*	*	*	*	*
Feminism (pro)	*	-.19	-.13	.16	*
Variance explained	19%	40%	32%	13%	9%

*Not significant.

66

are forced to rely on each other even more than they would in other parts of the country; therefore, they have a greater influence on one another's religion. If the family unit is the critical target of evangelization in the United States, then a fortiori it is of decisive importance in the big city.

The basic difference in explanatory models applied to the whole Catholic population and those applied to Chicago (Table 9) is that mass and communion in Chicago are more affected by the behavior of the spouse than they are in the rest of the country. Otherwise, there is virtually no difference in the betas for age, doctrine, sex attitudes, sermons, clericalism, and feminism— though in the United States as a whole, doctrine influences frequency of prayer and in Chicago it is sexual attitude which influences frequency of prayer. Also, in Chicago a combination of age, religiousness of spouse, doctrinal and sexual attitudes, attitudes toward sermons, and attitudes toward feminism explain two-thirds of the variance in religious behavior—a more than presentable achievement in any exercise of sociological explanation.

TABLE 9

ALIENATION IN CHICAGO AND UNITED STATES

(betas)

	Closeness to Church		Mass		Communion		Prayer	
	U.S.	Chi	U.S.	Chi	U.S.	Chi	U.S.	Chi
Age	.32	.09	.19	.10	.20	.11	.07	.13
Spouse's religiousness	.24	.13	.26	.47	.29	.38	*	*
Doctrine	.24	.10	.19	.15	.19	.13	.28	*
Sex attitudes	.17	.16	.10	.11	.17	.20	*	.19
Clericalism	*	.09	.11	*	*	*	*	*
Sermons	.18	.18	.14	.14	.10	.10	.10	.14
Feminism	*	*	.14	.11	*	*	*	*
Variance explained	37%	19%	27%	40%	30%	32%	13%	11%

Crisis in the Church

Conclusion

Who, then, are the alienated Catholics? They tend to be younger, from less religious families, to be married to less religious spouses. While such factors as doctrinal and sexual attitudes, sermons in their parish, the perceived leadership of the clergy, and feminism do have some effect on devotion/alienation, the principal explanatory resources available to us are age and family—family of origin and, more importantly, family of procreation. While the alienation problem is more serious among young people, the dynamics which affect their religious behavior are little different than those which affect the behavior of those over 30. The evangelization of the alienated, then, runs up against the stone wall of age and parental influence, about which the Church can do absolutely nothing, and the complex problem of the husband-wife relationship, which the Church must approach gingerly.

McCready and I hypothesized that the correlation between religiousness of spouse and one's own closeness to the Church would be highest in those marriages where there was the greatest satisfaction and lowest in marriages where there was less satisfaction. The data confirmed our suspicion. In marriages with low satisfaction levels, the correlation of closeness to Church and spouse's religiousness was *minus* .39; in marriages with moderate levels of satisfaction the correlation was *plus* .27; and in marriages with the highest levels of satisfaction the correlation was .50. The most religiously influential marriages are those with the highest levels of interpersonal satisfaction. Moreover, it is precisely in those marriages with the highest levels of satisfaction that the greatest closeness to the Church can be found. At the top level of marital satisfaction, 37 percent of our respondents ranked themselves as close to the Church, as opposed to 28 percent of those who were only moderately happy in their marriages. Furthermore, a third of those in the most satisfactory marriages reported that their spouses were very religious, as opposed to a fifth of those with only moderate levels of marital satisfaction. In other words, spouse's religious influence is strongest in the most satisfying marriages, and in such marriages spouse's influence "tilts" toward greater religiousness. Clearly the marital intimacy of husband and wife is a critical factor in any evangelization effort.

Thus sexuality, tossed out the front door by evangelization enthusiasts, comes in the back door: the more satisfying the relationship, the more influential it will be religiously, and the influence is usually in the positive direction, that is, toward making people more devout and less alienated. Improve the quality of marital intimacy and very likely the level of religious devotion will rise. Given the immense importance of spouse's religiousness on own religiousness, no sensible evangelization plan can afford to avoid the issue of intimacy. If intimacy is ignored, I suspect that most other evangelization efforts will not be very successful.

Chapter Three

WHO ARE THE "UNCHURCHED"?

THE "unchurched" seem to be the principal target for evangelization enthusiasm of both Catholics and Protestants. There is considerable vagueness about who the unchurched are. One has the impression from reading the literature of evangelization and listening to the conversations of would-be evangelists that the unchurched are a large group of Americans standing around waiting to be invited by organized religion to join up. All one needs to do, it would appear, is to approach them enthusiastically, proclaim the Good News, hand out parish census cards and collection envelopes, and the process is complete. The unchurched, then, are often pictured as men and women of good will and open minds; indeed, perhaps more good will and more open minds than many of the disaffected, the dissatisfied, and the alienated members of one's own denomination. Evangelization enthusiasts have many anecdotes to establish that there are such people in American society. Surely one would not deny that there are some Americans who need little more than an invitation to affiliate with a church. In fact, however, the available empirical evidence suggests that most of the unchurched are unchurched because they want to be, and enthusiastic evangelization among them is likely to have the same fate as the biblical seed which fell on the hard ground.

There are a number of different definitions current which purport to describe who these unchurched are—most of them not very precise. For the purposes of this chapter I will define the unchurched as those who either have no formal religious affiliation or those who go to church less than once a year. There are two NORC data sets which are pertinent for studying the unchurched. Both have advantages and liabilities. The NORC General Social Survey, conducted every year between 1972 and 1977, has a large data base (over 9,000 cases) but relatively few religious questions. On the other hand, the 1973 NORC Basic Belief study has a considerable number of religious questions which enable us to get at the religious orientation of the unchurched, but the case base is slightly under 1500. In this chapter we will adopt the strategy of using the General Social Survey (GSS) to describe social, demographic, and secular attitudes of the unchurched and the Basic Belief data to study religious orientation.

The laws of probability not having been repealed, the unchurched are 21 percent of both samples—18 percent attend church less than once a year and 4 percent have no religious affiliation (with some overlap). One-fifth of the American public, in other words, by this definition can be considered unchurched and hence targets for evangelization.

There are no socioeconomic correlates of being unchurched (Table 1). Income and education make no difference at all. The unchurched are somewhat more likely to come from large cities and their suburbs and less likely to live in small cities and villages, but the difference is not all that great. (Sixteen percent of the village population is unchurched, as opposed to 23 percent of the large city population.) Regional variety is somewhat more important, however. Southerners, particularly those from the east south central, are less likely than the typical American to be unchurched (18 percent from the south Atlantic region, 16 percent from the east south central, and 18 percent from the west south central). Westerners are much more likely to be unchurched (26 percent of those living in the mountain states and 32 percent of those living in the Pacific coast states). In fact, almost one-quarter of the unchurched living in the United States live in the mountain and Pacific regions.

TABLE 1

WHO ARE THE UNCHURCHED

(NORC General Social Survey)

Education	%		Region	%
No college	20 (6297)		North east	22 (430)
College	21 (2255)		Middle Atlantic	22 (1586)
Graduate school	22 (481)		East north central	21 (1923)
			West north central	18 (670)
Income	%		South Atlantic	18 (490)
Under $7000	21		East south central	16 (476)
$7000-$15000	21		West south central	18 (789)
Over $15000	21		Mountain*	26 (352)
			Pacific*	32 (574)
Size of Place	%			
Large city	23 (1496)			
Medium city	21 (762)			
Suburb of large city	22 (1252)			
Suburb of medium city	23 (441)			
Unincorporated SMSA	21 (1098)			
Small city	18 (484)			
Town	20 (509)			
Village	16 (294)			
Open country	20 (1129)			

*23% of all the "unchurched" live in the mountain and Pacific regions.

There are, then, relatively few demographic correlates with being among the unchurched. They are more or less evenly distributed through American society. In substantial part, however, the unchurched lack religious affiliation because they are very different from the churched in their religious convictions (Table 2). More than half of them do not believe in life after death, more than half of them do not believe that God's love is at work in the world, more than one-third do not believe they can find a

Crisis in the Church

fundamental meaning in life, 43 percent of them take an angry or pessimistic worldview (as opposed to 17 percent of the rest of the population), three-fifths of them pray less than once a week, two-fifths say they do not feel close to God, 47 percent say it is not important for the children to believe in God, 44 percent are not certain about their own belief in God, more than one-quarter see no purpose in life and no hope for the future, and more than four-fifths of the unchurched who are married are married to unchurched spouses. The unchurched, in other words, are not apples ripe on the tree for evangelistic picking by any stretch of the imagination.

TABLE 2

RELIGIOUS ATTITUDES AND BEHAVIOR OF THE "UNCHURCHED"
(Per Cent)

	"Unchurched"	Churched
Belief in life after death	54	31
Believe God's love at work in the world (no)	57	26
Believe can find a fundamental meaning in life (no)	35	5
Angry or pessimistic world view	43	17
Prays less than once a week	59	17
Spouse "unchurched"	82	14
Does not feel close to God	43	11
No purpose in life	26	13
God's love not in the world	28	4
Even in tragedy there is hope for the future (no)	27	4
Important for children to believe in God (no)	47	13
Believe in God (not certain)	44	29
Not certain what I believe	34	20
(Number)	(301)*	(1154)

*21% of the adult population.

They are also (Table 3) likely to be substantially more liberal both on sex attitudes and on abortion attitudes, to have lower levels of confidence in the clergy and not to believe in life after death. (The negative correlation between life after death and being unchurched is −.26 in the GSS and −.23 in the Basic Belief survey.) The problem, then, with clerical leadership and liberal views on sex, which the Catholic Church faces among its own membership, will not go away in any evangelization of the unchurched, who are likely to be even less accepting of the traditional sexual ethic than the Catholic rank and file.

TABLE 3

(NORC General Social Survey)

Age	−.11
Sex	−.11
Education	*
Sex attitude scales	.27
Abortion attitude scale	.25
Confidence in clergy	−.22
Belief in life after death	−.26

Just as lower levels of religious devotion are rooted in part in the past of a person, so, too, is his entry into the ranks of the unchurched. The mother and father of the unchurched person are both less likely to have gone to church and less likely to be joyous in their religious style than those of other people. In addition, there is a greater probability that the father of an unchurched person himself had no religious affiliation (Table 4); and the unchurched person remembers himself as being less religious both as a child and a teenager than those who are religiously affiliated. The largest factor predicting whether a person

75

TABLE 4

CORRELATES OF "UNCHURCHED"

(NORC Basic Belief Study)

Step 1

Mother's church attendance	-.18
Father's church attendance	-.18
Mother's religious joy	-.15
Father's religious joy	-.15
Father unaffiliated	-.12
Mother unaffiliated	*
Region west	.10

Step 2

Religiousness as child	-.10
Religiousness as teen	-.17

Step 3

Spouse "unchurched"	-.48

Step 4

Psychological well-being	-.12
Marital adjustment	-.10

Step 5

Angry world view	-.24
Faith**	-.23

* no statistical significance

** A combination of belief in life after death and belief that God is behind everything that happens.

is unchurched is whether his wife is also unchurched—a .48 correlation between his own membership among the unchurched and one's spouse's belonging in the same category.

Finally, the unchurched have higher levels of personal unhappiness and marital maladjustment than do the rest of the population. They are more likely to react angrily to the problems of life and death and less likely to believe in life after death and God's providence than other Americans.

Not only are the unchurched less likely to accept the Church's teaching on sex and abortion and more likely to be anticlerical, they also come from less religious families, are very likely to be married to an unchurched spouse, and differ sharply from churched adults in their interpretation of the meaning of human life. One must conclude that the unchurched choose to be unchurched—and not because they have been neglected by organized religion.

The eleven variables in the NORC Basic Belief study which enter meaningfully into the explanation of whether a person is unchurched are assembled in the flow chart of Figure 1. Altogether they account for almost two-fifths of the variance, thus explaining a substantial part of why some Americans are unchurched. The most powerful predictor is spouse's religiousness (beta of —.42), but, in addition, the happiness of marriage (−.10), religious faith (−.18), one's religiousness as an adolescent (−.10), and whether one lives in the west (.06) all related directly as to whether one is in the ranks of the unchurched or not. Family background variables are absorbed at earlier stages in the model and exercise (with the exception of one's religiousness as a teenager) their influence indirectly, particularly through the faith and religiousness as a teenager intervening variable—41 percent of the religiousness of a person as a teenager can be explained by family background religious variables. Unfortunately for a deeper understanding of why people are unchurched, the two strongest predictors—faith and spouse's church attendance—are themselves poorly explained by prior variables in the flow chart: only 10 percent of the

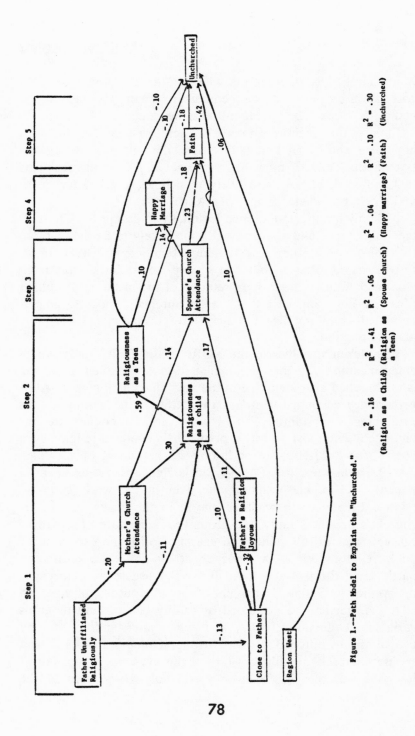

Figure 1.—Path Model to Explain the "Unchurched."

$R^2 = .16$ $R^2 = .41$ $R^2 = .06$ $R^2 = .04$ $R^2 = .10$ $R^2 = .30$
(Religion as a Child) (Religion as (Spouse church) (Happy marriage) (Faith)   (Unchurched)
                       a Teen)

variance in faith and only 6 percent of the variance in spouse's church attendance are accounted for by prior models.

The unchurched are likely to come from unreligious families, to be married to unreligious spouses, and not to accept basic religious propositions as true. Any attempt to evangelize them must take into account these very serious obstacles.

Spouse's religiousness is absolutely critical. Family background variables account for 6 percent of the variance; when teenage religiousness is added, 7 percent of the variance is explained (Table 5). Then, when spouse's church attendance is added, 18 percent more of the variance is explained, leaving only 5 percent additional variance to be attributed to marital happiness and faith. If you want to evangelize a member of the unchurched, therefore, you are going to have to evangelize his/her spouse at the same time.

TABLE 5

VARIANCE EXPLANATION OF "UNCHURCHED" ADDED AT EACH STEP IN THE MODEL

		Added	Total Explained
1.	Family background	6 %	
2.	Childhood and teenage religiousness	1 %	7 %
3.	Spouse's church added	18 %	25 %
4.	Marital happiness	1 %	26 %
5.	Faith	4 %	30 %

In the NORC General Social Survey, attitudes toward the clergy, life after death, sexual permissiveness, and abortion explained 14 percent of the variance of the unchurched (Figure 2). Since only the life after death attitude overlaps with the Basic Belief study model in Figure 1, it is reasonable to speculate that if the two models could be combined in one set of data, somewhere between 40 and 50 percent of "unchurchedness" might be accounted for by the fifteen variables in the combined model—approximately half by the single factor of spouse's religiousness.

Figure 2--Variance Explained by Religious Attitude Model--NORC General Social Survey.

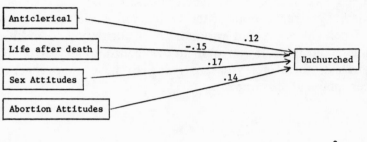

$$R^2 = .14$$

A fifteen-variable model combined from Figures 1 and 2 is obviously a very complicated affair. Indeed, many of the interrelationships among the variables would be hard to imagine even if the lines were drawn on a page and numbers were attached to them. However, the combined model, even if its explanatory power is highly successful by social science standards, would in fact be less complex than the reality of "unchurchedness." In particular, the subtle interrelationships between spouse's religiousness and faith and attitudes escape not only our ability to diagram but the capacity of the data to capture. For example, how do a couple work out a joint attitude on life after death? Apparently there is a disposition for them to be similarly religious—or similarly unreligious. They may not agree on human survival beyond death, but they certainly exercise considerable influence on each other in religious behavior and presumably in conviction about survival (which correlates with religious behavior), which conviction in its turn affects the couple's religious behavior and probably is affected by it. It hardly needs to be said that we know virtually nothing about the dynamics by which religious convictions emerge in the marriage relationship and how these convictions fit in with other aspects of the marriage—especially the sexual. Any "evangelization of the unchurched" which is not based on a more sophisticated knowledge of the role of religion in marriage and marriage in religion than what is presently available to us will be little more than an exercise in groping in the dark.

However, Catholic "evangelists" should be aware that for many of the unchurched the Catholic position on sexuality (and abortion) will be a serious obstacle—even more serious than it is among its own dissatisfied active members.

Obviously the most important question a group embarking on an evangelization campaign should ask itself has to do with dynamics of the mutual religious influence of husband and wife. Unfortunately, it is very difficult to untangle the complexities of this question, and the data available to us do not enable us to provide much of an answer. If one takes one's own description of subjective religiousness as a dependent variable and one's spouse's religiousness as intervening variable, and then considers only variables from family background, one can create a model such as those that exist in Figure 3. Indeed virtually all the high explanatory power of the three models in Figure 1 can be attributed to the religiousness of the spouse. We have no clear notion based on precise research of how important religiousness is in the choice of spouse, or, more precisely, to what kinds of people religiousness is important. We have no notion at all of what subtle chemistry is at work in creating the religious atmosphere of the family; there does seem to be, however, some difference in the dynamics at work for men and women. The "joyousness" of parents affects both one's own religiousness and the religiousness of one's spouse. Men, in other words, who come from religiously "joyous" families are more likely to choose religious

Figure 3.—Models for Subjective Religiousness.

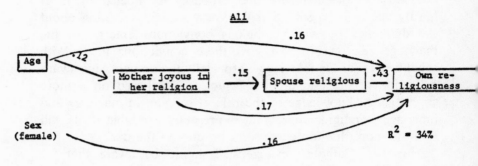

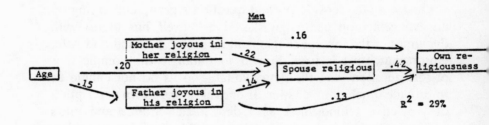

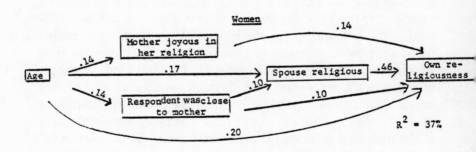

spouses. The father's religiousness has no effect at all for women either on their own subjective religiousness or the perceived religiousness of their husbands.

Given the fact that religiousness of spouse is important for both men and women and important for objective and subjective religious behavior, we would like to understand what influences are important in the choice of religious spouse. However, the

TABLE 6

SPOUSES RELIGIOUSNESS DOES NOT RELATE

TO

Happiness of parents' marriage

Happiness of respondent's youth

Parents' religious devotion

Educational attainment

Number of years in Catholic school

Attendance at Catholic colleges

Positive influence of priest and nuns in early years

Number of Catholic friends

Living in a Catholic neighborhood, now or as a child

Living in the same neighborhood now as when a child

"Sexual revolution" variables

Living in a neighborhood with your ethnic group

Religious experiences

Does relate significantly, however, to marital satisfaction

	Men	Women
gamma =	.08	.48

answer to such inquiries will apparently have to await more detailed research on the religious behavior of young people and the religious decisions a couple makes at the time of marriage for, as we note in Table 6, spouse's religiousness does *not* relate to a very considerable number of the variables that one might have expected it to on theoretical or substantive grounds. However, marital satisfaction is much higher among women who have religious husbands and somewhat higher for men with religious wives.

TABLE 7

STANDARDIZED COEFFICIENTS BETWEEN RELIGIOUSNESS OF ROLE OPPOSITES
AND OWN RELIGIOUSNESS (CATHOLICITY FACTOR) FOR
SELECTED AMERICAN ETHNIC GROUPS

(Betas)

	Irish	German	Italian	Polish
Mother	--	.25	--	--
Father	.33	--	.13	.26
Spouse	.48	.30	.28	.19

Interestingly enough, the importance of the religiousness of the spouse varies greatly among American Catholic ethnic groups (Table 7). The standardized relationship between spouse's religiousness (with mother's and father's religiousness and education and sex held constant) and CATHOLICITY (a scale that measures mass attendance, communion reception, various kinds of organizational and devotional activities and contributions) is almost .5 for the Irish (explaining one quarter of the variance), .3 for the Germans and Italians (explaining 9 percent of the variance) and .2 for the Poles (explaining 4 percent of the variance). In the family life of Irish Catholics, then, the influence of the spouse is enormously more important than it is in the families of other Catholic ethnic groups (exactly the opposite is true, incidentally, of alcohol consumption—the spouse has no influence on the average in the Irish family and substantial influence in other families).

In three of the groups there is also a statistically significant standardized correlation between CATHOLICITY and father's religiousness—though the correlation is twice as high for the Irish and the Poles as it is for the Italians. But in the remaining German group, the beta for mother's religiousness is significant, for father's religiousness it is not significant. Fathers, in other words, influence the religiousness of their offspring to some extent if they are Italian, and more if they are Irish or Polish; mothers do not influence their offspring in those ethnic groups. Among Germans, however, it is mothers who have the influence, not fathers. Finally, while the spouse is by far the most influential religiousness factor for the Irish, Germans, and Italians, the father is more important among Poles.

TABLE 8

STANDARDIZED COEFFICIENTS BETWEEN RELIGIOUSNESS OF ROLE OPPOSITES
AND OWN RELIGIOUSNESS FOR MEN AND WOMEN BY SEX
FOR SELECTED AMERICAN ETHNIC GROUPS

(Betas)

| | Men | | | |
	Irish	German	Italian	Polish
Mother	.16	.12	--	--
Father	.15	--	.36	.30
Spouse	.41	.43	--	.27
	Women			
Mother	--	.19	.19	--
Father	.40	--	--	.49
Spouse	.50	.45	.48	.15

Crisis in the Church

Even though there are no differences between men and women in the importance of the spouse's religious influence in the whole Catholic population, the picture is considerably more complex when one looks at the various ethnic groups. The spouse has virtually no religious influence on Italian males but substantial influence on Italian females, while, on the other hand, Polish men have more influence on their wives than do Polish wives on their husbands. Mothers influence Irish and German men and German and Italian women. Fathers do not influence German men and women or Italian women (Table 8). Note that Poles are influenced only by fathers and that the father's support is more important than the spouse's for both sexes, but particularly among women. Italians are influenced by opposite sex parents, Germans by their mothers, the Irish by their fathers (though Irish men less so than Irish women—in part, perhaps, because the former are also influenced by their mothers).

There are no available explanations for these differences in the ethnic group literature, but these suggest that if the relationship between the spouses is the critical religious influence in the life of an American Catholic and if the object of evangelization should be the family, and particularly the husband-wife relationship, then a somewhat different style of evangelization is appropriate for different ethnic groups within Catholicism—and, in all probability, non-Catholic ethnic groups as well. Evangelization, therefore, is even more complicated than this volume has made it appear. (Even though I earn my living by studying ethnicity, I would not have thought of looking at the ethnic influence on spouse's religiousness had it not been for the suggestion of Dr. Mary Durkin.)

In the unlikely event that those attempting to engineer an evangelization campaign are interested in more research, the most important subject on which they could focus is the mutual religious influence of husband and wife. You simply cannot understand the religious behavior of a married American, whether it be devotion, an unchurched condition, religious disidentification, or alienation (as we shall see in later chapters), unless you also understand the religiousness of the spouse and how the family's approach to religion grows, develops, and orients itself. If the relationship between the husband and the wife is as important as it appears to be in the first two chapters of this book (and nothing that happens in the rest of the book will cause us to change our evaluation), the Catholic Church with its virtually nonexistent credibility in matters of sexual ethics is in an awkward position to mount any enthusiastic evangelistic campaign. To evangelize the individual you must evangelize the couple; but to evangelize the couple means to raise questions about the marital relationship, and to raise questions about the marital relationship inevitably raises questions about sexuality. But the Church lacks credibility in sexual matters even with its members, and the unchurched are, if anything, even more "liberal" on sexual issues than are members of the Church. Obviously, evangelization efforts should not be abandoned, but there should be no illusions about the obstacles.

The unchurched, then, tend to be nonreligious in terms of doctrine, liberal in terms of morality, and nonreligious in both family of origin and family of procreation. Some of them, doubtless, are ready candidates for an evangelization campaign; most of them are not, and only the naive enthusiast would deceive himself by thinking differently.

Chapter Four

WHO ARE THE DISSATISFIED?

THE unchurched are those who belong to no particular denomination or attend church once a year or less; the alienated are those who remain within the denomination but are marginal in their religious practice; the dissatisfied, with whom this chapter is concerned, are those who object to the quality of services being provided by their local congregation. Dissatisfaction is a form of alienation, and for some people it may lead to more serious alienation. Furthermore, since bishops and priests cannot evangelize by themselves, in any evangelistic effort lay dissatisfaction with the services being rendered by a parish will make it more difficult to recruit potential associates and colleagues in such activity.

There has been considerable discussion in American Catholicism about "experimental" parishes and about "new parish" models. This experimentation, however, is not valid because no criteria are set up beforehand by which to measure success or failure (save for the "feelings" of the clergy and religious who preside over the "experiment"). While the testing of new models of parish ministry is certainly important in the work of the Church, the transition to new models is likely to be a slow process. In the interim most people will be served by existing institutions. Therefore, it is appropriate to determine what are the factors which make for satisfaction with existing parishes—especially since it seems unlikely that any new model or any

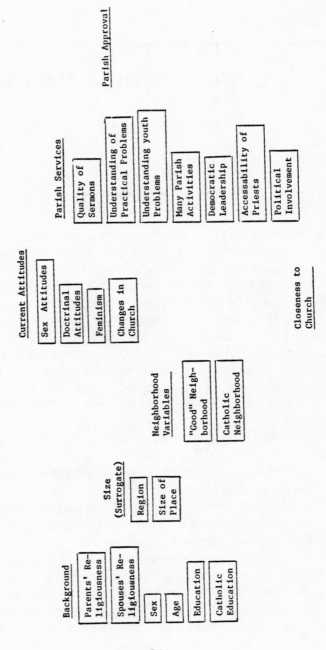

Figure 1--A Model for Parish Approval.

90

experimental parish will seem attractive to the laity if it does not do at least as well those things which seem to correlate with success in existing models.

The model in Figure 4.1 reflects a consideration of both the data available in the 1974 NORC survey and the kinds of variables which theoretically might be expected to correlate with approval of the parish. There are six different "blocks" of potential influence:

1. *Background*—either remote or proximate. These variables represent those things out of the past which a person brings to his interaction with his/her age, educational attainment, number of years in Catholic school, sex, and the religiousness of both parents and spouse.

2. *Size of the parish.* Much of the literature both in Europe and the United States about the "ideal" parish insists on the need of small communities in which the pastor and the people can know each other well. While small parishes seem to be humanly more desirable than large ones, there has not been, as far as I know, any evidence advanced to support the notion that there is a greater level of satisfaction in small parishes than in large parishes. Unfortunately, the 1974 NORC study did not ask questions about the size of one's parish. However, both region of the country and size of place might serve as roughly approximate "surrogate" variables for size, since presumably parishes will be smaller in small towns than they will be in large cities and since presumably in the mostly non-Catholic South parish communities will not be as large as they are in the heavily Catholic North.

3. Size and backgrounds are "givens." Another set of factors which might affect parish approval are the attitudes on *certain religious and social issues* of Catholics, attitudes which are a result of the more or less free choice of the specific respondent— attitudes on sex, on religious doctrines, on feminism (as a measure of liberal-conservative orientation) and on the changes in the Church.

4. At the same "level" in our model is the respondent's

description of how close he is to the Church. It might be argued that the parish has a very notable impact on the self-definition of a person as to how close he is to the Church and belongs farther to the right as a dependent variable. But for this chapter it is moved into the middle of the model on the assumption that closeness to the Church is a factor "external" to the actual functioning of the parish. We are assuming, in other words, that the respondent comes to his parish encounter with his closeness to the Church self-definition already achieved. It makes more sense to put closeness to the Church in a prior position to parish approval so that the impact of subsequent variables—parish services—may be free of the influence of one's definition of being close to the Church.

5. Finally, in the third level of factors there is a block of neighborhood variables: whether a given parishioner considers the neighborhood in which he lives a good place in which to dwell and the proportion of Catholics in a neighborhood. It is at least theoretically possible that the better the neighborhood, the more satisfied the parishioner will be with his parish and the more Catholic the community, the more satisfactions and pressures there may be for parish approval.

6. The last block of variables has to do with parish services, sermons, the priest's understanding of practical problems, his understanding of youth problems, the perception of the parish as being "active," the democratic leadership, the accessibility of priests, and the political and social involvement of priests.*

------

* Democratic leadership is based on the item asserting that most priests expect lay people to be followers. The political item index is made up of two items dealing with sermons on social issues and political activism on the part of priests. Neither of these items necessarily applies just to the respondent's parish but rather they deal with all priests (the previous four variables are all specific to respondent's parish). The item for accessibility of priest is in response to the question, "Have you had a serious conversation about religion with a priest during the past two years?" It could just as well, of course, measure the respondent's persistence in seeking out a priest as the availability of a priest.

Thus in the model in Table 1 we have specified twenty-two variables which may affect attitudes of Catholics towards their parish and specified the order in which these variables might operate. It remains to define parish approval. There is in the 1974 study no specific question about whether a Catholic likes his parish or not. However, a combination of two items seems to give a fairly satisfactory indicator of parish approval. The first item asks whether the parishioner approves of the way his pastor is doing his job—an adaptation of the Gallup item used to measure approval of presidential performance. When faced with this question, 82 percent of American Catholics expressed approval of the performance of their pastor (higher than their approval of the Pope, the bishop, or any president the country has ever known). Distribution of responses in this item made it a mathematically unsatisfactory indicator. However, of the 82 percent who endorsed their pastor's performance only 18 percent carried that endorsement into action by being active in a parish organization. If, then, membership in a parish organization as a form of action and approval of the pastor's job performance as a form of attitude are combined, one gets a neat, "normal" population distribution, a scale in which 18 percent are "high" (active and approving), 64 percent are "medium" (approving but not active), and 18 per cent are "low" (not approving). Thus, our parish approval scale is a combination of reaction to the pastor's job performance and parish activity.

Table 1 shows what correlations exist between three theoretically specified variables and the parish approval index. The largest R's are to be found in the parish service block—.41 with sermons, .52 with practical problems, .42 with youth problems, .22 with the rating of the parish as "very active", and .23 with democratic leadership of the clergy. Closeness to Church also has a high correlation (.4). In the background block of variables only age (.18), spouse's religiousness (.12), and parents' religiousness (.11) show modest correlations with parish satisfaction. There are also modest correlations between parish satisfaction, on the one hand, and sex attitudes (.17), doctrinal

TABLE 1

CORRELATIONS WITH PARISH APPROVAL INDEX

Background Block

Parents' religiousness	.11
Spouse's religiousness	.12*
Age	.18
Sex	**
Educational attainment	**
Years in Catholic schools	**

Size (Surrogate) Block

Region (South)	**
Size of place	**

Current Attitudes Block

Sex attitudes	.17*
Doctrinal attitudes	.19*
Feminism attitudes	**
Approval of changes in Church	**

Closeness to Church .40

Neighborhood Block

"Good" neighborhood	.17*
Catholic neighborhood	**

Parish Services Block

Sermons	.41
Practical problems	.52
Youth problems	.42*
Parish activities	.22
Democratic leadership of clergy	.23
Social activism of clergy	**
Church open during day	**
Conversation with priest during past two years	**

*Correlation significant but becomes insignificant in multi-variate model. All *variables together account for less than .1 of the variance in multivariate model.

**Correlation not statistically significant.

attitudes (.19), and whether the neighborhood is rated as "good" (.17). Only about half of the variables, in other words, turn out to be significantly related with parish satisfaction. In the previous chapter, we saw that personal devotion was heavily influenced by background variables and by current attitudes, but parish satisfaction seems much more influenced by the de facto performance by the parish of a number of critical services.

It will be insisted, as it normally is in the face of social research findings, that it is only common sense that activities, counseling skills, sermons, and leadership style would have notable impact on parishioners' satisfaction with their parishes. Doubtless this is the case, but then one wonders why such common sense is not applied to the training of seminarians, in-service training of priests, the selection of pastors, the evaluation of clerical effort, the determination of agenda for clergy professional meetings, and campaigns and enterprises to influence the effectiveness of the American Church. If the importance of counseling, sermons, activities, and leadership is as great as common sense seems to have told us, why has so little been done to upgrade our performance in these areas?

When all the variables which had a significant effect on parish approval were put into a multiple regression model, some two-fifths of the variance in parish approval was explained—an impressive performance for social science research of this sort. The beta coefficients for five variables—spouse's religiousness, sex attitudes, doctrinal attitudes, handling of youth problems, and a "good" neighborhood—all declined beneath the level of statistical significance (the "youth problem" variable was heavily correlated with the "practical problem," and its high correlation coefficient was obviously a mask for the more basic and fundamental "practical" problem concern). Removing these five variables from the model diminished its explanatory power by less than one percentage point, so they can safely be ignored in further discussion of parish satisfaction. The final regression equation (Figure 2) involves seven variables which together explain 39 percent of the variance in parish approval.

TABLE 2

PARISH APPROVAL IN CHICAGO AND UNITED STATES

	United States	Chicago
Background		
Parents' religiousness	.11	.12[a]
Spouse's religiousness	.12[a]	.22
Age	.18	.18[a]
Sex	*	*
Education	*	*
Years in Catholic school	*	*
Current Attitudes		
Sex	.17[a]	.21
Doctrine	.19 [a]	.23a
Feminism	*	-.09[a]
Approval of changes in the Church	*	*
Closeness to Church	.40	.22[a]
Parish Services		
Sermons	.41	.30[a]
Practical problems	.52	.57
Youth problems	.42[a]	
Parish activities	.22	
Democratic leadership of clergy	.23	.21

[a]Correlation significant but becomes insignificant in multivariate model. All variables[a] together account for less than .1 of the variance in multivatiate model.

*Not statistically significant.

We have previously found that "background" variables were more important than "current" attitudes in explaining religious devotion. The exact opposite, however, is the case with parish satisfaction. The three variables external to the parish—age, parents' religiousness and (hypothetically in the present case) closeness to Church—only account for 17 percent of the variance, while the parish services block accounts for an additional 22 percent even when the impact of the background variables is already put into the model. People not unsurprisingly approve of their parishes when parishes do well those things which people think are important—sermons, priestly skills in dealing with practical problems, a high level of church activities, and democratic leadership. We have no data from the past, but one wonders if the findings reported in Figure 2 would have been all that different ten, fifteen, twenty, fifty years ago in the American Church. People like their parishes if the sermons are good, if the priests are sensitive and understanding, if they are democratic in their leadership style, and if they have a busy, active parish. They don't like parishes where the priest is autocratic, where there are few activities, where the counseling is poor and the sermons are bad.

One can draw from this brief analysis two practical conclusions. First of all, any effort to intensify the evangelization activity of the American Church and to improve the performance of the American parish must take into account such simple bread-and-butter issues as sermons, counseling, parish activities and leadership style. Few human institutions other than automobile and cosmetic manufacturers get such clear and precise feedback from their clientele as to what they want. American Catholics want high quality sermons, sympathetic counseling, active parishes, and democratic leaders. The finding is, as remarked earlier, self-evident, commonsensical, obvious, and banal— which is why so much is currently being done to improve sermons, counseling, leadership style, and parish activities.

It is worth noting, incidentally, that since the sermon question was first asked in the Ben Gaffin *Catholic Digest* study in 1952,

Crisis in the Church

Catholics rated their clergy higher than did Protestants and Jews in preaching performance and ability to handle problems. In 1965, they rated them lower than Protestants and Jews. In 1952, 43 percent of American Catholics described the sermons as "excellent;" in 1974, this had declined to 23 percent. In 1952, 72 percent said their clergy were "very understanding" in dealing with practical problems; in 1974, it had fallen to 48 percent. In other words, the Catholic clergy is rated more poorly today than it was in the past (even the recent past) on precisely those areas of professional competence which correlate most strongly with parishioner satisfaction. We are apparently getting worse and worse at the things which matter most (or, if not getting worse, at least perceived as doing more poorly).

A second practical conclusion would be that in any search for transitional parishes or for new models one must take into very serious account the demand of the ordinary Catholic for good sermons, democratic leadership, a high level of parish activities, and sympathy and understanding in dealing with practical problems. It may well be assumed that the "new model" parishes would automatically do all of these things well. On the basis of the present performance of the clergy—not excluding the liberal, progressive clergy—such an assumption must be considered very tenuous indeed.

Parish Satisfaction in Chicago

Since the dynamics of alienation are the same in Chicago as they are nationally, one is not unprepared for the finding that there is relatively little difference between those things that make for parish satisfaction among American Catholics on the whole and in the Archdiocese of Chicago (Table 2). Spouse's religiousness is more important in Chicago in predicting satisfaction (as it was in predicting religious devotion), and self-defined closeness to Church is less important, as are sermons. There is also a statistically significant negative relationship between feminism and parish satisfaction in Chicago that does

98

Figure 2--Parish Approval.

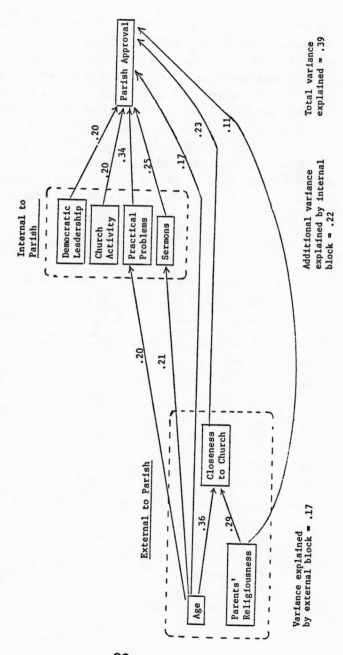

not exist nationally. Otherwise, Chicagoans are satisfied or dissatisfied with their parishes for about the same reasons that other American Catholics are with their parishes.

Our parish satisfaction model explains 39 percent of the variance for the country as a whole and 37 percent for Chicago. But still, when one looks at the standardized coefficients (Table 3), there are somewhat different dynamics at work in the country's largest archdiocese. Age, parental religiousness, and closeness to Church, all statistically significant variables in the national model, play no part in the dynamics of Chicago parish satisfaction, nor does the quality of sermons preached in Chicago.

TABLE 3

PARISH APPROVAL IN CHICAGO AND UNITED STATES--STANDARDIZED
RELATIONSHIPS WITH PARISH APPROVAL

(betas)

	United States	Chicago
Closeness to Church	.23	*
Parents' religiousness	.11	*
Age	.17	*
Sex attitudes	*	.13
Youth problems	*	.17
Parish activity	.20	.09
Sermons	.25	*
Practical problems	.34	.52
Democratic leadership	.20	.11
Variance explained	39%	37%

*Not significant.

Furthermore, parish activity and democratic leadership of the laity are less important in Chicago than they are nationally. However, sex attitudes and the priest's skill in working with young people have a statistically significant effect on parish satisfaction in Chicago, and the priest's skill in dealing with the practical problems of adults—the most powerful predictor of parish satisfaction in the country as a whole—is an even more important factor in parish satisfaction in Chicago. (The standardized coefficient is .34 nationally and .52 in the Archdiocese of Chicago.) Indeed, if one wished to improve the level of satisfaction with parish in the archdiocese, one could concentrate strategically almost all one's resources on improving the counseling skills of the clergy, because that factor is far more important than all the others put together. As will be noted in a subsequent chapter, the dissatisfaction with these skills on the part of the Catholic laity in Chicago is higher than it is nationally—ironic when one considers that professional training in psychological counseling began in the Archdiocese of Chicago more than twenty years ago, and Chicago probably has more professionally trained clerical counselors than any other archdiocese in the country. Further research on the state of the Archdiocese of Chicago ought to focus with great care on the issue of what the laity consider to be the skills required for understanding and sympathy among the clergy.

Conclusion

The alienated and the unchurched have been heavily affected by factors in their backgrounds—age, family of origin, family of procreation. It is relatively hard for the Church to deal with any of these influences directly. But the dissatisfied have been affected by influences over which the Church has substantial direct control—sermons, counseling skills, parish activities, and democratic clerical leadership. If a successful evangelization campaign depends in part on the enthusiasm of those already participating members of Catholic parishes, then it is reasonably clear what emphases should be chosen. It is quite easy to specify that evangelization within the parish community requires better leadership, preaching, and counseling skills among the clergy. While such skills are both teachable and learnable, they cannot, unfortunately, be acquired overnight or as part of a year-long evangelization program. However, such skills, if acquired, would be some kind of guarantee that those alienated and unchurched who are attracted by an evangelization campaign will not quickly join the ranks of dissatisfied persons.

Chapter Five

WHO ARE THE COMMUNAL CATHOLICS?*

WHEN the 1968 encyclical *Humanae Vitae* was issued there were two expectations of what the outcome would be. The right-wing expectation, confidently expounded by some Church leaders (perhaps many had their fingers crossed), was that the Holy Father had spoken, and those Catholics who were using birth control pills or other forms of contraceptives would stop. The left-wing expectation, heard in many liberal Catholic quarters, was that Catholics would continue to use birth control and leave the Church. While there has been a notable decline in religious devotion, there has not been an increase in disidentification from the Church because of the encyclical. The left and the right were both correct and incorrect. Catholics who practiced birth control did not leave the Church, but neither did they obey the Pope. They continued to practice birth control, according to liberal expectations, and stayed in the Church, according to conservative expectations. Both sides would consider them inconsistent, but such inconsistency does not seem to bother the ordinary Catholic lay person. In addition, then, to alienation, dissatisfaction and disidentification (about which more in a subsequent chapter), there is also another way of sorting out one's relationship with a religious denomination. One could call this form of dissidence "voluntarism."

---

* An earlier version of this chapter appeared in the international journal *Concilium*.

Crisis in the Church

By "voluntarism" I do not mean that church membership is voluntary. There being no established church in this country and no real inheritance of religious affiliation, church membership for American Catholics has been voluntary since its very beginning. I mean, rather, that American Catholics have discovered that it is possible to be a Catholic in the way one chooses, without regard for the "official" norms of Catholic behavior, as these are imposed either by the teaching Church through its hierarchical representatives or by the elite, liberal Church through bureaucratic agencies and journalistic media.

I have used the models of "communal Catholic" and "the two churches" before to emphasize different aspects of this new voluntarism.[1] The communal Catholic model suggests that many Catholics choose to be Catholics the way many Jews choose to be Jews: that is, they identify with the Catholic community, are interested in the Catholic heritage and tradition, wish to pass Catholicity on to their children, but do not look to the Church for meaningful instructions on how to regulate their lives. Some communal Catholics are devout, others not; but the critical point is that even the non-devout have no inclination to identify as anything else but Catholic and the devout have little inclination to yield much credibility to the Church as an official teacher.

My "two-church" model was proposed as an alternative to the two-church view of those who see one church as the bureaucratic hierarchy and the other as the liberal laity. I contend that a much more useful model compares the Church in the "neighborhoods" with the Church "downtown." The neighborhood Church is the Church at the parish level and beneath; the downtown Church is of the chancery office and above. Whether it be the Church of the conservative hierarchical bureaucracy *or* the Church of the liberal elites, the neighborhood Church doesn't pay much attention to either. It asks only that the downtown Church leave it alone. It does not look to the hierarchical Church downtown for guidance on birth control, and it does not look to the liberal Church downtown for guidance on racial attitudes and social problems. It pays little attention to either the *National Catholic Reporter* or *The Register,* either to *The Commonweal* or *Our Sunday Visitor,* either to the Washington and Chicago meetings of bishops or the Detroit meetings of the liberation theologians and the Call to Action. In fact, it is barely aware that these exist.

Essential to both these models is the assumption that a substantial proportion of the Catholic population is no longer listening to communications from elite levels, whether they be hierarchical or liberal intellectual. In both cases the rank and file Catholic either ignores or explicitly rejects the right of the elite to tell him or her what to do and how to live. Compliance with elite norms and directives, in other words, is part of the voluntary component of church affiliation.

The second assumption of both models is as critical as the first. The "communal" Catholic is free to affiliate or not to affiliate. When he affiliates he does so on terms of his own choosing, with little concern for the alleged inconsistency with which he is charged by the downtown elites. The failure of communication between downtown and the neighborhood is so complete that the neighborhood not only no longer listens to downtown, it even denies the *right* of downtown to establish norms.

A series of questions in the NORC Catholic schools study asked respondents whether the Church had the right to teach what position Catholics should take on certain issues. The two issues considered here are racial integration and birth control. The answers to these questions correlated at a sufficiently high level (.39) that they can be formed into an index called "communal Catholic."

Of the Catholics in the country, 85 percent reject the Church's right to teach on one or the other issue; 49 percent reject its right to teach on both them. Half the Catholics in the United States, in other words, deny the Church has the right to lay down what position Catholics should take on "proper means of family limitation" and "racial integration." The first of our two assump-

Crisis in the Church

tions fits the data nicely. Half the American Catholic population has turned off the "downtown" Chuch on both the "liberal" issue of racial integration and the "conservative" issue of birth control.

What impact does such a decision to reject the legitimacy of the Church's teaching have for these "neighborhood communal Catholics?" We must first inquire who they are and how they differ from those who accept the Church's right to teach. In fact,

TABLE 1

CORRELATIONS WITH "COMMUNAL CATHOLIC" SCALE

	Communal	All
Age	- .13	*
Education	*	.14
Sex	*·	*
Parents' religiousness	*	.10
Spouse's religiousness	*	.13
Papal infallibility	- .18	-.16
Approve of Pope Paul's job performance	- .15	*
Approve of bishop's job performance	- .12	-.09
Approve of pastor's job performance	*	*
Catholic friends	*	*
Catholic neighborhood	*	*
Approve of quality of sermons	- .18	.*
Catholic education	*	.13

*No statistically significant correlation.

(Scale made up of two items: rejection of Church's right to teach on birth control and on race.)

106

they are not very different from other Catholics (Tables 1 and 2). They are slightly younger (with a correlation of −.13), slightly less likely to approve of ecclesiastical authority (modest negative correlations with the acceptance of papal infallibility, approval of Pope Paul's job performance, approval of bishop's

TABLE 2

DIFFERENCES BETWEEN COMMUNAL CATHOLICS[*] AND ALL CATHOLICS

	Communal (per cent)	All (per cent)
Mass attendance (2 or 3 times a month)	54 **	61
Communion reception (2 or 3 times a month)	27	32
Pray privately every day	54	60
Pray privately every week	77	80
Would give more to support Catholic schools	77	80
Would give more than fifty dollars a year	57	60
Serious conversation with priest in last 2 years	19	20
Has thought of leaving the Church (no)	84	85
Belongs to parish organization	19	21
Sympathy for resigned priests (a great deal)	33	32
Read a spiritual book in last 2 years	28	33
Participated in religious discussion group in last 2 years	19	21
Attended "house liturgy" in last 2 years	5	8**

[*]Reject both birth control and racial teaching authority

**Communal Catholics significantly different from other Catholics.

job performance, and approval of the quality of sermons in their parish). In other respects the communal Catholics are no more likely to be better educated, to have less or more Catholic education, to come from non-religious families, to have Catholic friends and to live in Catholic neighborhoods. Nor is there any difference between men and women. The communal Catholics, in other words, are ever so slightly younger and somewhat more critical of the Church's authority, but in other respects (including such variables as ethnicity, region of the country, size of dwelling, morale, psychological well-being, church contributions, marital status), there are virtually no differences between them and other Catholics.

The communal Catholics, then, seem to be no different from other Catholics save that they reject the Church's right to teach on contraception and on race. (For instance, they are not even significantly different in their *de facto* racial attitudes.) Has this decision to reject the official teaching authority of the Church had much influence on their religious practice? Surely it would have been predicted beforehand that once one makes such a decisive break with an authoritative church, one's traditional religious practice will erode, but, as we note in Table 2, there is virtually no evidence of such an erosion. Indeed, there are only two statistically significant differences between those who reject both the birth control and the racial integration teaching authority and the rest of the Catholic population. The communal Catholics are somewhat less likely to go to church two or three times a month or more—though 54 percent of them still report that level of church attendance—and they are somewhat less likely to have attended a "house liturgy" during the last two years (5 percent for the communal Catholics; 8 percent for all Catholics), but a quarter of the communal Catholics receive communion two or three times a month, more than half pray every day, more than three-quarters pray every week, more than three-quarters would support Catholic schools, more than half would give in excess of fifty dollars a year additional support to Catholic schools if asked to do so, 84 percent have not thought of leaving the Church, one-fifth belong to parish organizations, more than a quarter have read a spiritual book in recent years, a fifth have participated in religious discussion groups, and a fifth have had serious conversations with a priest during the past two-year period. Neither in their background nor in their observable religious practice is there much difference between those Catholics who accept the teaching authority of the Church and those who reject it. However theologically and philosophically inconsistent it may be, a very substantial proportion of the Catholic population (about half) is able to reject ecclesiastical authority's right to teach authoritatively on race and on birth control and still maintain approximately the same levels of religious practice as do the general Catholic population.

One suspects that this finding will be greeted with disbelief and perhaps contempt by both the right-wing and the left-wing elites. As one Roman cardinal said to me, "It is too bad they don't have the faith anymore." And as a Pittsburgh monsignor said to me, "We are ashamed of Catholics in the ethnic neighborhoods." Shameful and unfaithful they may be, but apparently they don't realize it. They reject the Church's right to teach on birth control and race and still continue their routine Catholic behavior almost entirely unaffected by such rejection of teaching authority.

How can such inconsistency occur? First of all, one must note that there is no evidence at all that the people engaging in communal Catholic behavior think that they're being inconsistent. They obviously do not think that it is necessary for devout Catholicism to accept the Church's right to authoritatively teach on racial and sexual matters. Elite Catholicism may say, "But you have to accept our right to tell you what you should think about sex and/or race." It is the essence of voluntarism that the communal Catholic can respond, "That's what *you* say." You have your official models of Catholic behavior, in other words, and I have mine, and you can't make me live according to your model.

There has been a substantial increase in the number of communal Catholics since the first NORC study in 1963 (rising from 30 percent of the population to 50 percent). As in most other matters reported in *Catholic Schools in a Declining Church,* virtually all the increase in the number of communal Catholics can be acounted for by a decline in support for papal authority and a decline in endorsement of the Church's official birth control teaching (and none of it relates to the support for the changes in the Second Vatican Council). My colleagues and I concluded in *Catholic Schools in a Declining Church* that the dramatic decline in Catholic religious practices seem to be affiliated with the birth control encyclical *Humanae Vitae* (there was considerable supporting evidence from other data sets for this conclusion). It now also appears that the fundamental explanation for the increase in the number of communal Catholics is the reaction of a large proportion of the Catholic population to *Humanae Vitae*—a reaction which seems to have caught both the left-wing and the right-wing elites off balance. The right-wing elites predicted that once the Pope had spoken, the matter would be closed, and Catholics would abandon artificial birth control. The left-wing elites predicted that once the Pope had spoken, Catholics would leave the Church and continue to practice birth control. In fact, both were wrong: Catholics continued to practice birth control and stayed in the Church (for the most part). The principal effect seems to be declining levels of religious devotion, and an increase of those who reject the Church's right to be an authoritative teacher.

One should ponder for a moment that three-quarters of those who reject the Church's right to teach authoritatively on race and on birth control are still willing to increase their annual contribution for the support of a de facto exercise of the Church's teaching function in the Catholic schools, and that half are willing to give fifty dollars and more a year to support the exercise of that function in their parish. It is all right, in other words, it would seem, for the Church to teach, but in certain areas of the exercise of the teaching authority, the Church no longer seems to enjoy any *credibility* as a teacher. One may speculate, in the absence of data, that a substantial number of Catholics in the United States simply do not think the Church is believable when it speaks on race or sex because it is their impression that the Church does not know what it's talking about: It does not understand the problems of marital intimacy and child rearing; it does not understand the problems of racially changing neighborhoods, of urban crime, of deteriorating schools, inflation, increasing taxes and decline of governmental services. If people have made up their minds that you do not know what you're talking about, you can talk until you are blue in the face and you will have no impact at all. You can claim to speak for God, or, alternatively, for the enlightened Christian conscience. The implicit response from the communal Catholic is that God knows what He's talking about but you don't, so why should he believe you are speaking for Him? One may insist until Judgment Day that one is speaking for God, but if people deny that basic assumption, they will simply tune you out and turn you off.

The Communal Catholic in Chicago

Just as half the Catholics in the country are "communal," so are half the Catholics in the Archdiocese of Chicago. However, they are significantly less likely to receive communion two or three times a month than the noncommunal Catholics (but still 8 percentage points more likely to receive it two or three times a month than the national communals). They are also significantly less likely to say they would give more to support Catholic schools, though three-quarters of them are still willing to contribute. There is, in addition, a statistical difference between communal and noncommunal Catholics in Chicago in organizational membership—noncommunal are more than twice as likely to belong to parish organizations. But in other matters—mass, private prayer, conversations with the priest, not having thought seriously of leaving the Church, contributions to the Church, contributions to keep one's own parish school open, and strong

111

sympathy for a religious vocation in the family—Chicago communal Catholics are no different from noncommunal ones (Table 3).

TABLE 3

COMMUNAL CATHOLICS IN CHICAGO AND UNITED STATES

(Per cent)

	Communal U.S.	Communal Chicago	Noncommunal Chicago
Mass attendance (2 or 3 times a month)	54 %	59 %	66 %
Communion reception (2 or 3 times a month)	27	35	49*
Pray privately every day	54	57	61
Would give more to support Catholic schools	77	75	83*
Serious conversation with a priest during past 2 years	19	18	23
Had thought seriously of leaving the Church (no)	84	82	82
Organizational membership (parish)	19	14	29*
Approve of son a priest	--	63	60
Approve of daughter a nun ·	--	52	56
Proportion of income contributed to Church	--	1.9	2.1
Proportion would give to poor parish to keep school open	--	0.2	0.2

* Statistically significant.

Educational attainment and the number of years attending Catholic school (Table 4) correlate negatively with being a communal Catholic in Chicago, though they do not do so nationally. Spouse's and parental religiousness both have a significant influence in Chicago, which they do not have nationally. Even though Chicago's cardinal archbishop is not very popular in his diocese, the relationship between approval of bishop's job performance and whether one chooses to be a communal Catholic is virtually the same in Chicago as it is in the rest of the nation.

TABLE 4

COMMUNAL CATHOLICS IN CHICAGO AND UNITED STATES
(Correlations)

	Chicago	United States
Age	*	-.13
Education	-.14	*
Sex	*	*
Parental religiousness	-.10	*
Spouse's religiousness	-.13	*
Papal infallibility	-.16	-.18
Approval of Pope Paul's job performance	*	-.15
Approval of pastor's job performance	*	*
Sermons	*	*
Catholic school attendance	-.13	*

*Not statistically significant.

If one constructs a model that takes into account Catholic school attendance, educational attainment, parental and spouse's religiousness, acceptance of papal infallibility, and approval of the cardinal's job performance (Table 5), one can explain a mere 7 percent of the variance between the communal and the non-communal Catholics. These six factors, in other words, are all statistically significant but very modest in their impact.

TABLE 5

VARIANCE EXPLANATION OF COMMUNAL CATHOLICS IN CHICAGO

Catholic school	-.08
Education	-.10
Parental church attendance	-.09
Spouse church attendance	-.09
Papal infallibility	-.12
Approve cardinal's job performance	-.09
Variance explained	7%

In Chicago, as in the rest of the nation, the communal Catholic is little different from his more authority-sensitive confrere either in his origins or in his present level of religious practice. Discouraging as it may be to Church leadership, it is clear that about half the Catholics in the country, as well as half in the Archdiocese of Chicago, have cheerfully decided that they can ignore the Church leadership on specific issues and remain contentedly in the Church.

Conclusion

While voluntarism is another way of distancing oneself from institutional leadership if not from the institution, it is unlikely that a direct assault on voluntarism would be helpful in a program of evangelization. On the contrary, an attempt at this time by ecclesiastical authority to reassert its right to claim obedience might be counterproductive for evangelization. More likely, however, it would be simply a waste of time. Those who have determined not to listen will continue not to do so until those to

114

whom they are supposed to be listening reacquire credibility. This is not an impossible task and is probably a necessary prelude to any serious and responsible exercise in evangelization. However, in any attempt to reacquire credibility, the leadership must realize it has lost it. So the first order of business is not to evangelize but to regain credibility. Only when you are credible to your own most devout membership can you hope to become credible to those outside.

Chapter Six

WHO ARE THE "DISIDENTIFIED"?

THE literature of religious "disidentification"* generally offers three different kinds of explanations for the phenomenon of people withdrawing from the religious denomination in which they were raised:

1. *The secularization model.* In the form advanced by Glock[1] and his students "secularization" means that the, more sophisticated, the better educated, and the more cosmopolitan people become, the less likely they are to maintain their ties with their traditional religious affiliations or with any religious affiliation at all. Wuthnow[2] has reexamined this explanation and found it deficient in many respects. A more popularized form of the secularization model can be found in the thinking of many religious leaders. Whatever factors lead people to the fringe of

---

* "Fallen away," "lapsed," and "apostate" are words that will not be used in this chapter. Each might be considered objectionable to some readers, and the alternative word, "disidentification," is the most accurate, given the data on which this chapter is based.

Four questions asked in five national General Social Surveys conducted by the National Opinion Research Center (NORC) form the basis for the analysis here reported: (1) the respondent's religious identification now, (2) his religious identification at age 16, (3) respondent's spouse's religious identification now, and (4) respondent's spouse's religious identification at age 16. A "disidentifier," in the meaning used here, is someone who identified with a given denomination at the age of 16 and does not do so now.

a denomination will lead them out of the denominations when they become powerful. A person will drift into the low levels of religious devotion because, let us say, of dissatisfaction with the sexual ethic or of the racial stance of his denomination, and then when his dissatisfaction grows stronger will drift across the line separating the identifier with the disidentifier.

2. *The family strain model.* Most of the serious research done on the phenomenon of religious disidentification (by Kotre, Zelan, Caplowitz, and Greeley)[3] emphasizes the powerful influence of family background in the decision to disidentify religiously. The church, as Kotre has pointed out, is an institution which emits many stimuli. Which stimulus one chooses to focus on in determining to identify or disidentify is a function of the psychological perspective one brings from the family experience to one's encounter with the church. Living apart from one's family and coming from a "broken" family or a family in which there is conflict or in which there is unusual strain between a person and his parents are powerful predictors of religious disidentification. Similarly, the religious disidentifiers are likely to be dissatisfied and unhappy personally and to take strong liberal stands on political and social issues. Zelan and Caplowitz suggest that an ideology of political liberalism may become a substitute religion for them.

3. *The religious intermarriage or "musical chairs" model.* This explanation, contained in one essay by the present author and much of the research literature on Jewish intermarriage, recognizes that the American population plays a game of religious musical chairs at the time of marriage. Men and women rearrange their religious affiliations to minimize the strain and conflict which might exist in a family because of different religious loyalties. In such a game of musical chairs, religious conviction, faith and unbelief, devotion and loyalty are less important than minimizing family conflict. The conversion will usually be in the direction of the more devout of the two marriage partners.

There has been relatively little research done on either religious disidentification or religious exogamy in recent years.

Caplovitz's monograph on disidentification is concerned basically with young people who graduated from college in the early 1960s. The Jewish exogamy studies focus on that denomination and show mixed and conflicting findings. However, the NORC General Social Survey has asked questions about present and past religious identification for four of its five annual surveys, as well as a number of other questions which enable us to test each of the three explanations offered above for religious disidentification.

Questions about age and education will enable us to examine the Glock model of secularization. Questions about sexual attitudes and belief in life after death will permit us to examine the variant of the secularization model which sees disidentification as a continuous behavior linked logically with low levels of religious practice. Questions about whether the respondent lived with both parents at age 16, about trust, psychological well-being, and political disaffiliation will enable us to examine the family strain/disaffiliated personality model. Finally, questions about the religious affiliation of spouse at 16 and at the present time will enable us to investigate the musical chairs model.

Briefly, the most plausible explanation for the religious disidentification phenomenon is religious exogamy—an especially powerful explanation for Catholics. There is also some support for the other explanations, though virtually none for the Glock secularization thesis. It is true that both the young and the better educated are more likely to disidentify religiously, but this can be explained by increased exogamy and an increase in the level of general societal disaffiliation.

The analysis in this chapter suffers from all the handicaps described in previous chapters. In addition it has certain weaknesses of its own.

1. To say that disidentification is connected with exogamy does not mean that one has a clear notion of how the two relate to one another. Not all disidentifiers marry out of their denominations and not all participants in exogamous marriage disidentify. Where the two phenomena do occur, one does not know whether

disidentification came before the marriage or after it, and whether, if it came before, it occurred immediately before the marriage, taking place with the marriage in mind, or was an earlier event which might have been accounted for by either of the other two explanatory models. Certainly in the present analysis we find that there are a substantial number of young unmarried people whose disidentification can be accounted for by an alienation/disaffiliation model. These young people, it seems safe to assume, are part of a special phenomenon that occurred in the late 1960s. There may have been among older generations a similar disidentification based on anger or disbelief; but if this disidentification occurred prior to a religiously mixed marriage, very little trace of it can be found among those who entered religiously mixed marriages and then disidentified. It would appear, in other words, that musical chairs is one way out of a denomination—more of a response to the religious convictions of one's spouse—while religious alienation, for reasons either of conviction or a general tendency toward disaffiliation, is another way out with relatively little linkage between the two. Nonetheless, since we are dealing with a phenomenon that occurred sometime between the sixteenth birthdays of our respondents and the present, the most we will be able to do here is to speculate about the connections. A much more detailed study of the religious maturation process between the late teens and the late twenties would be required for more precise information and precise explanations of the complex link between religious identification and marriage.

There is, however, substantial evidence indicating that young people make up their minds about their religious affiliation at about the same time they make up their minds about their political affiliation—sometime between 17 and 30. (It is worth noting that the generation that grew up in the 1960s tends to have suspended ultimate decision about both these affiliations.)

2. The questions in the General Social Survey that are pertinent to our analysis are at least as good as items ever available for the study of disidentification and exogamy in the past. Nonethe-

less, they leave something to be desired. In a study explicitly designed to study disidentification, better operational indicators would surely have been designed.

For the analysis in the present paper the following variables were routinely built into the mathematical models: age, sex, respondent's education, respondent's spouse's education, respondent's parents' education, region of the country, city size, personal psychological well-being, marital adjustment, whether one lived with one's mother and father at 16, belief in life after death, church attendance, approval of extramarital sex, premarital sex, the distribution of birth control information to teenagers, belief that most people can be trusted, support for prayer and bible reading in public schools, confidence in religious leadership, support for the legalization of marijuana, and certain "anomie" items about marital status, whether people can be trusted to be fair, and whether life is exciting or dull.

3. As will be evident, the issues explored in this chapter are extremely complicated. For purposes of simplicity of presentation, correlational analysis is used most of the time. One of the disadvantages of using correlation/multiple regression is that when the distribution of respondents is skewed (for example, only one-sixth of our respondents have disidentified religiously), the correlation coefficients are likely to be relatively small and to obscure important relationships that nonparametric statistics would reveal. The problem is even more serious when the distribution on the second variable (area of the country in which the respondent lives) is also badly skewed. Thus evidence was found to sustain the conviction that religiously mixed marriages are more likely for Catholics who live in the south and the west than for those who live in the northeast and north central regions of the country. However, since only a relatively small proportion of the Catholic population lives outside of the northeast and north central regions, the regional variable is not a powerful explanation of religious disidentification (because most religious disidentification for Catholics still occurs in the north, where most Catholics live). Similarly, disidentification rates are high among

those who were not living in an intact family at age 16. Again, only a relatively small proportion of the population did not live in intact families; therefore, an unintact family (with one important and notable exception) is not an important explanation for religious disidentification. Most religious disidentification in fact occurs among those who came from intact families. When one chooses between parametric and nonparametric statistics in an analysis like this one, one realizes that there are costs and advantages to both techniques. The costs in a decision to use parametric statistics here are a loss of some interesting and useful information; but the benefits include a much clearer, orderly, and systematic presentation of a subject matter which is complicated enough to begin with.

TABLE 1

DISIDENTIFICATION RATES AMONG AMERICAN DENOMINATIONS[*]

(Per Cent)

Affiliation at Age 16	Current Affiliation					
	Protestant	Catholic	Jew	Other	None	Total
Protestant (3961)		3.4	0.1	0.7	5.5	9.7
Catholic (1625	8.5		0.4	0.4	7.2	16.5
Jew (150)	2.7	0.7		1.3	11.3	16.0

[*]Proportion religious affiliation at the age of 16 who no longer claim that affiliation.

Table 1 shows 10 percent of those who were Protestants at the age of 16 are no longer Protestants, while 16.5 percent of the Catholics and 16 percent of the Jews have disidentified with their denominations. (Jews are omitted from the analysis of the present chapter because 150 respondents are not sufficient for generalizations in an area in which there is intensive research being carried on by other scholars. There are not sufficient numbers for most of the Protestant denominations to permit detailed analysis—though, as we will note later, Baptists have a lower mixed marriage rate than other Protestant denominations. The Baptist-non-Baptist dichotomy, however, was not statistically significant in any other of the models constructed for this chapter.)

Sixteen percent of those who were Protestant at the age of 16 contracted marriages with spouses who were also Protestant at the age of 16. (It does not follow necessarily that either was still Protestant at the time of marriage.) Thirty-nine percent of Catholics contracted such exogamous marriages, as did 16 percent of the Jews (Table 2). However, when one looks at the present exogamy rates, one notes that they fall to 11 percent for Protestants, 23 percent for Catholics, and 10 percent for Jews. In other words, the game of religious musical chairs, by which spouses reduce exogamy rates by religious change, cuts by one-third Protestant and Jewish exogamy rates and cuts almost in half Catholic exogamy rates.

TABLE 2

EXOGAMY RATES AMONG AMERICANS

(Per Cent)

Denomination	Religion at Age 16	Present Religion
Protestant	16	11(2724)
Catholic	39	23(1025)
Jew	15	10(97)

Two-fifths of those who were Catholic at 16, in other words, married people who were not Catholics; but only about one-quarter of those who are Catholics today are married to people who are not Catholics today. Some of those who were Catholic at 16, in other words, have become non-Catholic; others remain Catholic and their spouses who were non-Catholic at 16 have become Catholic.* The net result of the rearrangements of religious affiliation in association with exogamous marriages is a 2 percent loss in total membership for Protestants and à 7 percent net loss for Catholics (Table 3). In other words, while 9 percent of those born Protestant disidentify, 7 percentage points of that disidentification is compensated for by conversions—most in association with religiously mixed marriages—and while 16.5 percent of those who were born Catholic have disidentified, 10 percentage points of that change are compensated for by converts—again, most of them in association with religiously mixed marriages.

TABLE 3

"SURVIVAL" RATES FOR PROTESTANTS AND CATHOLICS (NET LOSS—"MUSICAL CHAIRS" HAS BEEN PLAYED)

Protestant	Catholic
2%	7%

Disidentification is closely related to exogamy (Table 4). For both Catholics and Protestants, only 6 percent who married a spouse who was the same religion as they were at 16 have disidentified, while 30 percent of those who married out of their denomination have disidentified. Disidentification, in other words, is five times as high in exogamous marriage as it is in endogamous marriages. About one-fifth of both denominations who were

---

* It is possible, of course, that some of these "converts" to Catholicism became Catholic before marriage and independently of it. Our data do not enable us to examine this possibility, but it seems reasonable to assume that the number is not large. There were also a few respondents whose spouses converted to their religion and they themselves disidentified. This group is too small for the present analysis and is excluded from it.

never married have disidentified. Whether, if they were to marry, such respondents would reidentify with their old religion, identify with a new one, or remain disidentified is at best a matter of conjecture. However, most of the unmarried disidentifiers are young, and, as we shall suggest later in the paper, there seems to be a special dynamism at work among the disidentifying young.

TABLE 4

DISIDENTIFICATION RATES FOR MARITAL GROUPS
(% Disidentifying)

	Protestant	Catholic
Never married	18	21
Married in	6	6
Married out	30	30
Widowed	7	12
Separated	20	21
Divorced	13	12

Exogamy accounts for 50 percent of Catholic disidentification and 34 percent of the Protestant disidentification (Table 5). One-quarter of Protestants married to other Protestants have disidentified while only 13 percent of the Catholics married to other Catholics have disidentified. Approximately four-fifths of the married Catholics who have disidentified entered religiously exogamous marriages, as opposed to 56 percent of the disidentifiers among married Protestants in religiously mixed marriages. Among Protestants and Catholics, then, an absolute majority of the married disidentifiers are in religious mixed marriages—more than half the Protestants and almost four-fifths of the Catholics. Beyond any question at all, the exogamy explanation of disidentification is clearly the most powerful. But the question remains as to whether there are dynamics at work which lead to both disidentification and mixed marriage. Do people enter mixed marriages because they have disidentified, or are there two separate paths out of religious denominations, one through mixed marriage and one that may lead to mixed marriage but would operate independently of mixed marriage?

TABLE 5

DISIDENTIFICATION AND MARRIAGE

(Per Cent)

	Protestant	Catholic
Never married	21	23
Married in	27	13*
Married out	34**	50***
Separated, widowed, and divorced	18	16
Total	100 (385)	100 (257)

*Three percentage points of this group, however, have been divorced in the past, although they are now married to Catholics. If these are added to the marriage related disidentifiers, 84 per cent of those who were raised Catholics and are presently married but who have disidentified have done so in connection with a religiously mixed marriage or a divorce.

**56 per cent of the disidentifiers among the married.

***79 per cent of the disidentifiers among the married.

Table 6 details how the musical chairs game is played. Eighty percent of those who were Protestant at 16 married others who were Protestant at 16; four percent married spouses with Protestant identification at 16 but have themselves disidentified (a disidentification independent of marriage). Five percent entered religiously mixed marriages and now disidentify; another 4 percent have entered religiously mixed marriages, but their spouse

TABLE 6

RELIGIOUS DISIDENTIFICATION AND MIXED MARRIAGES

(Per Cent)

Spouse's Religion at 16	Self-identi-fication Now	Spouse's Identi-fication Now	Protestant Re-ligion at 16	Catholic Re-ligion at 16
In	In		80	56
In	Out		4	4
Out	Out		5*	12
Out	In	In	4**	8
Out	In	Out	7***	20
TOTAL			100(2751)	100(1066)

* Convert to other faith

** Spouse converted

*** Existing mixed marriage

127

became Protestant so that now the marriage is endogamous. Finally, 7 percent of the Protestants entered marriages which then and now are religiously exogamous, in which neither the respondent nor the spouse changed religious identification. It is the third and fourth categories, then, which represent the religious musical chairs—5 percent of the Protestants marry out of the denomination and move out of it, 4 percent move out but the spouse moves into the Protestant denomination—a net loss of 1 percent.

For Catholics the mixed marriage rates are much higher—44 percent of American Catholics marry persons who were not Catholics at 16. Twelve percentage points of this group disidentify with the Church, but another 8 percentage points are in marriages in which the spouse has converted to Catholicism, making it a net loss of 4 percentage points to American Catholicism because of religious intermarriage. Twenty percent of those Catholics who entered religiously mixed marriages are still in religiously mixed marriage with no change in spouse or self. Conversion as a result of mixed marriages among Catholics is more likely than disidentification, and a continuation of the marriage as mixed is even more likely.

There are almost a bewildering number of possibilities. Why do people enter mixed marriages? Why do people disidentify if they are not in mixed marriages? Why do some of the exogamously married disidentify? Why do some "convert" their spouses, and why do some remain in marriages which continue to be religiously mixed? What impact does "marriage conversion" have on denomination? Are those who were converted in association with marriage as "devout" as the "born" members of the denomination? How do those who switched in association with marriage compare with those who were devout members of the "sending" denomination, that is to say, the denomination they left behind? The answer to each question assumes a different comparison, a comparison that is logically designed to provide an answer. Table 7 presents the six questions, the comparison groups on which the search for answers will be based, and the list of figures or tables which present the results of our analysis.

TABLE 7

COMPARISONS IN THIS RESEARCH

Question	Groups Compared	Fig. or Table
1. Why do those who are not in religiously mixed marriages disidentify?	The unmarried and endogamously* married, disidentifiers versus nondisidentifiers.	Fig. 1
2. Why do people enter religiously mixed marriages?	The endogamously married versus the exogamously* married.	Fig. 2
3. Why do some exogamous marriages correlate with disidentification?	Exogamously married who remain exogamous compared to those in which self disidentifies.	Fig. 3
4. Why do other exogamous marriages correlate with conversion of the spouse to self's religion?	Exogamously married who remain exogamous compared to those which endogamy has been achieved by conversion of spouse.	Fig. 4
5. How religious are "marriage converts" in the new denomination?	"Converts" in question 4 compared with members of "receiving" denomination in endogamous marriages.	Table 8
6. How religious are "marriage converts" compared to old denomination?	"Converts" in question 4 compared to endogamously married in "sending" denomination.	Table 9

*
Endogamously married are defined as those whose religion at 16 is the same as the described religion of spouse at 16.

**
Exogamously married are those whose religion at 16 is different from that of described religion of spouse at 16. Disidentification of self or conversion of spouse (as measured by present religion question) may have happened before marriage, at the time of marriage, or after it.

129

Crisis in the Church

The first question has to do with that minority of disidentifiers whose decision is not related to a religiously exogamous marriage. The analytic variables available to us enable us to explain 14 percent of the disidentification of Protestants and 17 percent of the disidentification of Catholics when one compares the unmarried respondents or endogamously married respondents who disidentify with the unmarried respondents and the endogamously married respondents who do not disidentify. For Protestants there are no statistically significant relationships in the multiple regression model between nonmarital disidentification and demographic variables, such as age, education, sex, region (Figure 1-A). Three of the predictors of disidentification have to do with religion—confidence in religious leaders, belief in life after death, support for prayer and bible reading in the classroom—while three have to do with "moral" issues—premarital sex, extramarital sex, and legalization of marijuana. A generalized disaffiliation as measured by being a political "independent" also relates to Protestant disidentification, but only indirectly through the two "blocks" of religious and moral issues. Nonmarital disidentification for American Protestants, then, insofar as it can be explained by the tools available to us, seems to be a rather straightforward religious and moral disenchantment. Obviously, there are other factors at work (an R^2 of .14 is not large), but as far as our theories and analytic tools are able to be used on the question of nonmarital disidentification, it would seem that Protestants disidentify for religious and ethical reasons.

Among Catholics, the religious and ethical reasons are also at work—indeed, somewhat more strongly. There is a —.21 relationship between confidence in religious leaders and disidentification and a .17 between support for the legalization of marijuana and disidentification (Figure 1-B). There are also direct relationships between disidentification and age (—.1), education (—.11), general disaffiliation (.10), and divorce (.18). The three most powerful predictors of disidentification among Catholics whose disidentification is not related to religiously mixed marriage are a previous divorce, low confidence in

Figure 1-A—Nonmarital Disidentifiers for Protestants*

$R^2 = .14$

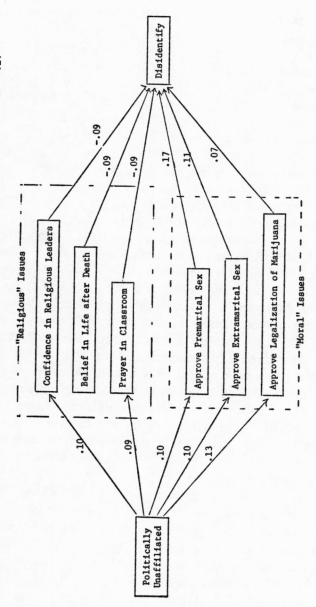

*Unmarried respondents or respondents who married within their own denomination but nonetheless disidentify compared to those who are unmarried or married within their denomination but who have not disidentified

NOTE: In all figures only statistically significant parameters are presented. Dotted lines are occasionally added for symmetry.

131

the clergy, and political liberalism as represented by support for the legalization of marijuana. The rather complex model in Figure 1-B really has two separate subsystems, a religious subsystem at the bottom of the model that involves divorce, belief in life after death, and confidence in religious leadership, and a "secular" subsystem at the top of the model that involves age, education, "unaffiliation," and support for the legalization of marijuana. Younger Catholics, better educated Catholics, Catholics who are political independents, and Catholics who support the legalization of marijuana are more likely to disidentify, as are Catholics who have been divorced, who have a low level of confidence in religious leadership, and who do not believe in life after death. Among that minority of Catholic disidentifiers whose disidentification is not marriage associated, both the first and the second models described in the beginning of the paper (the secularization model and the alienation model) seem to apply. The secularization model applies in two forms—age and education on the one hand and a continuation of problems with the clergy and religious conviction on the other. (Confidence in religious leadership can be taken as a rough equivalent indicator of attitudes toward clerical performance and life after death as a rough equivalent indicator of attitudes toward doctrine. It is worth noting that sexual attitudes, while tested, were not strong enough in their influence on Catholic disidentification to be included in this model—or in fact any of the models presented in this paper for Catholics, save that a previous divorce may in some indirect sense represent an indicator of sexual attitudes.)

The data available to us in this analysis do not provide much illumination on the question of why young people choose to marry outside of their religious denomination. For Protestants intermarriage is more likely to occur among the young and in the metropolitan areas of the north and less likely among Baptists. The Catholic picture is more complicated. Polish, German, French, and English Catholics are more likely to enter religious intermarriage than Irish, Italian and Spanish-speaking Catholics. They are also more likely to enter religiously mixed marriages

Figure 1-B—Nonmarital Disidentifiers for Catholics

$R^2 = .17$

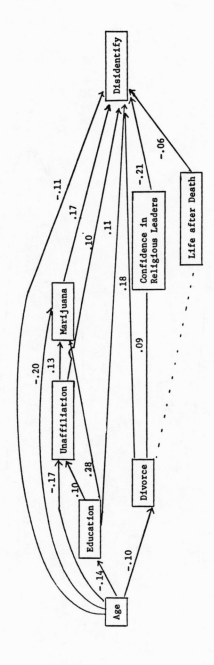

Figure 2—Religiously Mixed Marriages*

PROTESTANT

$R^2 = .06$

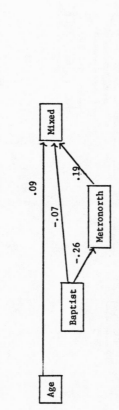

CATHOLIC

$R^2 = .08$

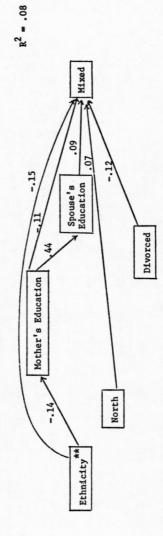

* Comparison between those who married spouses of the same religion at the age of 16 and those who married spouses of different religion at age 16.

**Irish, Italian, Latino

134

if they are from the south and if there is a previous divorce in their marital experience. There is no connection between their own education and religious intermarriage, but both their mother's and spouse's education correlate positively with religious intermarriage. Thus the better educated your mother is and the more education your spouse has, the more likely you are to enter an exogamous marriage if you are Catholic. Perhaps if you have a better educated mother you are more likely to be in a social environment in which there is more mixing between Protestants and Catholics and perhaps also, better educated women as potential marriage partners. Region plays a part for both Protestants and Catholics. Denomination for Protestants and ethnicity for Catholics are roughly parallel factors for both groups.

We can give only a meager answer to the question of why people enter religiously mixed marriages, even though such marriages in their turn are a substantial answer to the question of why people disidentify from the denomination in which they were raised. The data available for this analysis provide virtually no information on the childhood, familial, or religious experiences of our respondents, and it ought not to be expected that we would be very successful in explaining choice of marriage partners. The critical question of this paper is not why people enter religiously mixed marriages but rather why some of those who do disidentify with their denomination. One must compare those who entered exogamous marriages and remained in their denomination without their spouses converting and those who enter religiously exogamous marriages and disidentify with their own religion (Figure 3).

For Protestants this identification correlates positively with education. The better educated a Protestant is in the exogamous situation, the more likely he is to disidentify. Also, there is a surprisingly high correlation between not living with both parents at the age of 16 and disidentifying (.23). Finally, those Protestants who have left their own denomination in association with a mixed marriage are much more likely to report a higher level of marital happiness than those who remain Protestant in

135

Figure 3—Disidentification as a Result of Exogamy*

PROTESTANTS

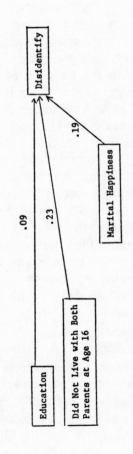

$R^2 = .08$

CATHOLICS

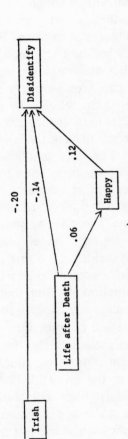

$R^2 = .05$

*Exogamously married who disidentify compared to exogamously married who do not.

136

religiously mixed marriages. One gets a hint from the first panel of Table 3 that respondents who had rather unhappy and troubled childhoods find happiness in the marriage they have entered. It is possible that this combination of unhappy childhood and deep satisfaction in a relationship with a spouse leads one to disidentify with one's original religion and join that of the spouse. It could be also that the sharing of values that results from religious conversion in this particular case (not in any other comparisons) leads to a higher level of marital happiness.

The model explaining Catholic disidentification in exogamous marriages is completely different. There is a large negative correlation of —.20 with being Irish. (Thirty-eight percent of those Catholics in religiously mixed marriages whose spouses have not converted disidentify with Catholicism. However, only 15 percent of the Irish in such marriages disidentify, the only group that is statistically different from any of the others. The Irish are less likely to enter mixed marriages, and once they have entered them, they are much less likely to disidentify.) There is also a —.14 relationship between belief in life after death and disidentification for Catholics and .12 between personal psychological well-being and disidentification. Catholic disidentifiers, in this particular set of circumstances, are no more likely to describe their marriages as happy than those who do not disidentify, but they are more likely to describe themselves as personally happy—a phenomenon which may be roughly parallel to the marital happiness described by Protestant disidentifiers.

In the introduction to the chapter we raised the possibility that there were two quite different systems of disidentification at work among Americans, one applying to those who entered religiously mixed marriages and the other applying either to the unmarried or to those who entered endogamous marriages. To test the accuracy of this suggestion one need only compare Figure 3 with Figure 1. None of the variables in Figure 3 for Protestants appear in Figure 1, and only one of the variables, belief in life after death, is in both Figure 1 and Figure 3 for Catholics. Figure 1 presents a picture of religious and moral crisis for

Crisis in the Church

Protestants and alienation and disaffiliation for Catholics. Figure 3, on the other hand, seems to present a picture of personal and marital psychological well-being, ethnicity for Catholics, and broken family for Protestants. While we still can explain only a relatively small amount of the variance, there seems little overlap in the reasons why the exogamously married disidentify and the reasons why others disidentify. Religiously mixed marriages do not seem to produce the kind of disidentification that can be considered a religious crisis, while the disidentification of the unmarried and the endogamously married does seem to correlate with a set of variables that could be described as religious crisis.

Nevertheless, the explanatory power of Figure 3 is disappointingly small given the fact that religiously mixed marriage is the most important explanation of religious disidentification. One would still like to know more of why some people in mixed marriages disidentify and others do not. One possibility would be that the explanation for disidentification lies less with the respondent himself (him/her-self) than it does in the respondent's spouse. Might it not be that the musical chairs at the time of exogamous marriage is a response to the religious needs, demands, or convictions of the spouse with the stronger religious commitment? Perhaps one should look at the matter the other way round, looking not at those who disidentify but rather at the spouses of those who convert.

We are not able to look at the spouses of the disidentifiers in our sample since the sample is not a study of families but of individuals. However, there are individuals in the sample whose spouses have disidentified with their religion of origin and joined the respondent's religion. It is therefore possible to ask how those whose spouses convert differ from those in mixed marriages in which the spouse does not convert, the two people continuing to live together with two religious commitments (Figure 4). The spouses of the converts are patently far, far more devout than the spouses of those who do not convert—a beta of .41 with church attendance for the spouses of those who converted to Catholicism and one of .32 for spouses of those who converted to Protes-

Figure 4—"Marriage Conversion"* (Spouse Joins self's Religion)

PROTESTANTS

$R^2 = .13$

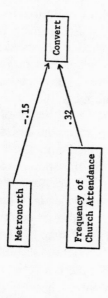

CATHOLICS

$R^2 = .22$

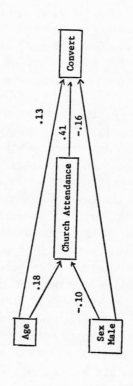

*Comparison between exogamously married whose spouse does not join self's religion (and self does not disidentify) and exogamously married whose spouse does join self's religion.

139

tantism. Those outside the metropolitan north are more likely to have spouses who converted to Protestantism; older Catholics and women Catholics are more likely than younger Catholics and male Catholics to report that their spouses have converted.

We do not know, of course, whether the high level of church attendance reported by the spouses of converts was a cause or a result of the conversion, since all we know is church attendance at the present time and not church attendance at the time of the marriage. It could be that the mutual and self-conscious reinforcement of religious values that comes from a "marriage conversion" leads the spouse to higher religious devotion than he/she would otherwise have had. However, it is certainly valid to speculate that the high level of religious practice observed among the spouses of converts reveals a deep religious commitment which existed also at the time of the marriage and which balanced the game of musical chairs in favor of the more devout partner. One may conclude tentatively that in religious disidentification associated with mixed marriage the important variables relate less to the marriage partner who disidentified and more to the marriage partner with whose denomination the spouse comes to identify. One converts to the religion of the more devout spouse. The religious crisis of a mixed marriage which leads to disidentification is not so much the crisis of lack of faith or commitment in one's own denomination as it is a crisis of stronger faith and commitment of the other person to his/her denomination.

It should not be thought, however, that the conversion is unauthentic or hypocritical, that the spouse merely goes along with the religion to which he/she has converted in order to keep the more devout member of the pair happy. There are few differences between those who were born Protestant or born Catholic and converts when it comes to religious behavior (Table 8). Indeed, Catholic converts are even more likely than born Catholics to believe in life after death (though Protestant converts are, as one would expect from Figure 3, less likely to believe in it than born Protestants). In terms of confidence in the clergy, church attendance, and sexual attitudes, converts and born members of denominations do not differ from one another at a level which achieves statistical significance. Converts are no less devout and, save for the Catholic belief in life after death, no more devout than those born in a denomination. However, those who have converted to Catholicism are not only more likely to report that they are happy in their marriage than those who have remained in religiously mixed marriages, they are also more likely to report that they are more happy in their marriages than are born Catholics who are married to other Catholics. Marital happiness among Catholics is more strongly affected by conversion than it is by initial endogamy.

TABLE 8

RELIGIOUSNESS OF CONVERTS[*]

(Gammas)[**]

	Protestant	Catholic
Church attendance	--	--
Life after death	-.32	.32
Confidence in religious leadership	--	--
Extramarital sex (approves)	--	--
Premarital sex (approves)	--	--
Birth control information for teens	--	--
Prayer in public schools	.37	--
Marriage happiness	--	.32

[*] Marriage converts compared to members of "receiving" denomination who are endogamously married and have not disidentified.

[**] Only statistically significant relationships shown.

Crisis in the Church

Furthermore, if one compares those Catholics who converted to Protestantism with those who remained Catholics, the converts are about as religious as those who remained Catholics. There is no statistically significant difference in church attendance. (Because of the small size of the number of converts, the 9 percentage point difference in weekly church attendance between converts to Protestantism and Catholics is not statistically significant.) Nor is there any significant difference in belief in life after death, and the marriage converts to Protestantism are significantly more likely to say they are very happy than Catholics who are still practicing Catholics. Those Catholics who have converted to Protestantism and those Protestants who have converted to Catholicism because of religiously mixed marriages, in other words, have not become unbelievers nor undevout; they have simply shifted the locus of their religious belief to another denomination—in all likelihood because the religious convictions of their spouse were stronger. The switch means greater marital happiness for those who convert to Catholicism and greater personal happiness for those who convert to Protestantism.

TABLE 9

RELIGIOUSNESS OF CATHOLICS WHO HAVE CONVERTED
TO PROTESTANTISM IN ASSOCIATION WITH
MARRIAGES COMPARED TO ENDOGAMOUSLY
MARRIED CATHOLICS

(Per Cent)

	Converts to Protestantism	Catholics
Weekly church attenders	41	52
Believing life after death	72	76
Very happy	61* (88)	40 .(609)

*Significantly different from Catholics.

142

The greater marital happiness for converts to Catholicism seems to be confined—at least as far as statistical significance goes—to Protestant men who have converted to the religion of their Catholic wives (Table 10). Nine-tenths of such men described their marriages as "very happy." On the other hand the bottom panel of Table 10 shows that the same cannot be said of Catholics, men and women, who have converted to the Protestantism of their spouses.

TABLE 10

HAPPINESS OF MARRIAGE AND CONVERSION

	Protestant converted to Catholicism and married to Catholics	Catholic married to Catholic
Male	89*(46)	72(291)
Female	74**(58)	65(319)

	Catholic spouse of Protestant convert to Catholicism	Catholic married to Catholic
Male	65**(43)	72(291)
Female	69**(39)	65(319)

	Catholics converted to Protestantism and married to Protestant spouse	Protestant married to Protestant
Male	65**(72)	71(1053)
Female	66**(69)	67(1140)

*Significant difference

**No significant difference

143

Crisis in the Church

Does this phenomenon of greater marital satisfaction among the men who converted to the Catholicism of their wives correspond to a higher level of satisfaction for their wives, that is to say, for the women whose husbands have converted to Catholicism because they (the wives) are Catholic? It should be noted that we are not dealing with the same couples but rather with national samples—and by now with a very small number of cases—of the two different categories, that is, male converts to the Catholicism of their wives and Catholic women whose husbands have converted to Catholicism. The middle panel of Table 10 does show, as one might expect if the higher level of satisfaction is shared by husbands and wives, that the Catholic women whose husbands have converted to Catholicism do report a higher level of marital satisfaction than Catholic women married to husbands who were always Catholic. But the difference (69 percent saying "very happy" for the former and 65 percent for the latter) is not statistically significant even though it is in the hypothesized direction. One therefore can say only tentatively that religiously mixed marriages which end up as Catholic marriages because of the conversion of the male partner to Catholicism produce the highest level of satisfaction (as perceived and reported by the respondent) of any marriages in the country.

To summarize the findings of the present chapter, one may make tentative answers to the six questions of Table 7.

1. *Why do those who are not in religious mixed marriages disidentify?* Protestants, insofar as our data provide answers, disidentify for religious and moral reasons; Catholics for religious reasons such as divorce, belief in life after death, and anger at the clergy, and also more general reasons of alienation, as measured by political nonidentification.

2. *Why do people enter religiously mixed marriages?* Baptists are less likely than other Protestants to do so; Irish, Italian, and Latino Catholics are less likely than other Catholics to do so. Younger Protestants and higher status Catholics (as measured by their mother's and spouse's educational achievement), as well as divorced Catholics, are more likely to enter exogamous marriages.

3. *Why do some exogamous marriages correlate with disidentification?* Marital happiness for Protestants and personal happiness for Catholics correlate with disidentification. Leaving the church of one's origin gives Protestants higher levels of marital happiness and Catholics higher levels of personal happiness. Those who grew up Irish Catholics are much less likely to disidentify in mixed marriages, and those Protestants who were raised in broken families are much more likely to disidentify as Protestants.

4. *Why do other exogamous marriages correlate with conversion of the spouse to self's religion?* The principal correlate of marrying a spouse who converts is one's own high level of church attendance—perhaps a reflection of the situation at the time of marriage in which the spouse was perceived as by far the more religious of the two and hence the one who determined the religious course the family would take.

5. *How religious are marriage converts in the new denomination?* Generally speaking, they are at least as religious as those who were born in the denomination.

6. *How religious are married converts compared to those in the denomination they left behind?* The answer seems to be that marriage conversion may lead to a shift in affiliation, but it does not lead to a change in religious devotion.

The last question is the most appropriate way, perhaps, to begin a final discussion of the various models proposed to explain religious disidentification. Quite clearly, mixed marriages are the major cause of religious disidentification. They have relatively little impact on the personal religious behavior of the people involved. Rather, they change the denominational situation in which the religious behavior occurs. A mixed marriage, in other words, may lead to a crisis of religious affiliation but not to a crisis of religious conviction or devotion. However, that kind of religious disidentification which occurs in a nonmarital and non-mixed marital context does seem to involve for both Protestants and Catholics a religious and moral crisis, a crisis which for Catholics, at any rate, seems to have some connection with a more general alienation. Those Catholics who disidentify outside the marital context seem to be influenced by explanatory variables not unlike those described in a previous paper as also affecting low levels of religious practice.

Is disidentification, then, merely a continuation of dynamics that are already at work in leading to low levels of religious practice? Does one drift to the fringes of the church and then if the factors affecting drift grow stronger, eventually drift out? The answer seems to be that such a process is indeed one way out, but a way out for only a minority of the disidentifiers. The other way is followed by the majority of Catholics who enter religiously mixed marriages in which faith and devotion do not change but affiliation does.

Finally, one must turn to the "secularization" explanation. Is it true that both youthfulness and education lead to higher rates of religious disidentification, which suggests that society is tending toward a higher level of religious nonaffiliation and indifference?

Table 11-A,B shows that those with college education and those under 30, both among Protestants and Catholics, are more likely to disidentify. For Catholics under 30, the disidentification rate is 21 percent: for Catholics over 30, 15 percent. For Protestants under 30, the disidentification rate is 15 percent: over 30, 8 percent. Virtually the same percentages apply to the difference between attenders and nonattenders of college. However, when one holds religious intermarriage constant, all statistically significant differences among age groups go away. If Protestants and Catholics under 30 are more likely to disidentify, the reason is that they are more likely to enter religiously mixed marriages. We have suggested before that since religiously mixed marriage represents a crisis of denominational affiliation and not a crisis of religious conviction, the secularization trend, insofar as it is measured by higher youthful rates of disidentification, is a trend which affects denominational affiliation, perhaps, but not religious devotion.

A control for exogamy also eliminates statistically significant differences between Catholics who attend college and those who don't, though a difference does remain among exogamous Protestants. (Thirty-six percent of the college attenders disidentify, as opposed to 16 percent of those who did attend college.)

It is interesting to note that among those who enter religiously mixed marriages there are no differences between Protestants and Catholics and between those under 30 and over 30—about three out of ten in all four categories of exogamous marriages disidentify.

TABLE 11-A,B

DISIDENTIFICATION BY AGE AND EDUCATION

(Per Cent Disidentifying)

A. AGE

| | Protestants | | Catholics | |
	Under 30	Over 30	Under 30	Over 30
All	15	8*	21	15*
Endogamous	7(363)	4**(1939)	9(117)	6**(535)
Exogamous	30(109)	28***(340)	31(101)	29**(314)

*Statistically significant difference from those under 30.

**No difference.

B. EDUCATION

| | Protestants | | Catholics | |
	College	No College	College	No College
All	15(1158)	8*(2793)	22(503)	14*(1118)
Endogamous	7(657)	3**(2642)	8(174)	6**(476)
Exogamous	36(140)	16*(309)	30(136)	30**(178)

*Statistically significant difference from college attenders.

**No statistically significant difference.

Crisis in the Church

Is the higher level of religious disidentification among the young part of a more general alienation syndrome that was the result of disturbances in American society in the late 1960s and early 1970s? It is well known that a large number of young people under 30 have not yet made a choice between the two political parties and continue to be political independents.[4] Nie, Verba, and Petrocik have raised the question of whether this group will ever be politically "mobilized." A parallel question is whether they will ever be religiously mobilized. The important question for the present paper is whether those who are unmobilized politically are also unmobilized religiously. Are the political nonidentifiers the same ones as the religious disidentifiers? Table 12 suggests that for Catholics, at any rate, they are. The politically affiliated Catholics under 30 are no more likely than the politically affiliated Catholics over 30 to disidentify religiously. However, it is precisely among those Catholics who are both under 30 and who are politically disaffiliated that one finds a rate of religious disidentification that is twice that of both their affiliated age peers and of their fellow disaffiliates over 30.

TABLE 12

AGE, RELIGIOUS DISIDENTIFICATION AND PARTY DISAFFILIATION
(Per Cent Disidentifying)

	Protestants		Catholics	
	Disaffiliate	Affiliate	Disaffiliate	Affiliate
Under 30	21*(406)	10*(432)	29*(238)	13**(224
Over 30	12(938)	7(2157)	16(406)	13(746

*Statistically significant difference from those over 30.

**Not statistically significant different from those over 30.

148

A similar pattern appears for Protestants. The highest dis-identification rate is among disaffiliates under 30. Among the affiliates, there is a statistically significant but very small (3 percentage points) difference between the younger and the older group.

Is mixed marriage or a more general nonaffiliation syndrome the more important predictor of religious disidentification for those under 30? Figure 5 shows that exogamy continues to be the strongest predictor, even for those under 30, of religious disidentification. But for Catholics there is also an independent

Figure 5—Political Disaffiliation, Exogamy, and Religious Disidentification among Those Under 30.

PROTESTANT

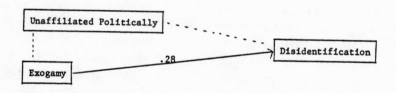

CATHOLIC

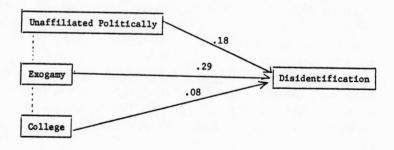

Crisis in the Church

contribution of college education (.09) and an independent contribution of societal nonaffiliation, as measured by the lack of a political affiliation. Alienation from societal institutions, in other words, does not seem to be a particularly pertinent factor in explaining disidentification of the young Protestants, but it does seem to be an influence on the disidentification of young Catholics—perhaps a sign of the acute institutional crisis which afflicted Roman Catholicism in the late 1960s and early 1970s.

By way of conclusion, what recommendations can one make for potential evangelists?

First of all, by far the largest number of those who have disidentified from the Roman Catholic Church have done so in association with religiously mixed marriages. They are happily married, devoutly practicing, believing members of Protestant denominations. They may have gone through a crisis of institutional affiliation, but they do not seem to have suffered any acute crisis of religious conviction. Attempts to "reclaim" them are not likely to be very successful or even very advisable.

Second, the 34 percent of Catholic disidentifiers who have not left in association with a religiously mixed marriage are perhaps a legitimate target for evangelization. Some of them have been previously divorced; there is also among them a tendency to resent the clergy, to doubt survival after death, and to be suspicious of all large social institutions. They are legitimate if difficult targets for reevangelization, and the difficulties should not be minimized. The techniques necessary to reevangelize them, however, should not be very different from those techniques necessary to reevangelize the still identifying but not practicing or infrequently practicing Catholics. It is worth noting, incidentally, that the Church's sexual ethic seems to be less a problem of those who have disidentified than it is among the nonpracticing who still identify.

There may be a third group, the young disidentifiers, who are both more likely to enter mixed marriages and also more likely to be politically unaffiliated (though there is no link, it would seem, between political alienation and the choice of a religiously

150

exogamous marriage). While the approach to both religious identification and mixed marriage among Catholics under 30 may well be different, surely the link between political nonaffiliation and religious disidentification is strongest among those under 30. (In fact it exists *only* among those under 30.) One finds here, then, another reason to urge that a study of Catholic adults under 30, including those who were Catholics at some time of their lives and are Catholics no longer, be undertaken by those who wish to embark on a program of evangelization.

Chapter Seven

THE LEADERSHIP ISSUE

Leadership in Crisis: Catholics in Chicago

Introduction

IN the first chapter I remarked that there were three advantages to having a detailed study of a specific diocese to parallel the national studies on which most of this book is based. The Chicago survey provides an opportunity to replicate the national model, it tests the possibility that religious dissidence may result from different factors in a large archdiocese, and it provides data to answer the question as to whether the quality and popularity of religious leadership has much short-run impact on the religious behavior of ordinary laity.

Most of the dissidence models tested in this book have been well replicated. Alienation, dissatisfaction, and voluntarism are roughly the same in Chicago as they are nationally, though parish services and religiousness of spouse seem to be even more important in Chicago than they are in the rest of the nation.

This chapter deals with the final question, does the popularity of the bishop have an impact on the religious behavior of the laity?

It is no secret that there has been conflict between Chicago's cardinal and the clergy of his diocese. (My own views on the matter are certainly on the public record.) The survey conducted by the *Chicago Tribune* in the summer of 1977 also made it clear that the cardinal is not very popular with the laity either. The question, then: What impact does an unpopular administration have on a large Catholic archdiocese?

Crisis in the Church

The Roman Catholic Archdiocese of Chicago is faced with a grave crisis of authority. Its cardinal archbishop is no more popular with Catholics than President Nixon was the year before his resignation. Pope Paul VI is respected, but a majority of Catholics question the doctrine of papal infallibility, and an overwhelming number flatly reject his teaching on artificial contraception. Parish priests are admired by the Catholic laity but receive very low marks on professional competence—in some cases significantly lower than in the rest of the country.

A random sample of Chicago Catholics (from Cook and Lake counties, which constitute the Archdiocese of Chicago) were asked the same question the Gallup Survey asks about the approval of presidential performance: "In general do you approve or disapprove of the way the cardinal, John Cardinal Cody, is handling his job?" Forty-two percent expressed approval, 33 percent disapproved, and 25 percent responded that they did not know. This was opposed to 82 percent approval rate for their parish priests, a 68 percent approval rate for the mayor of their municipality, and a 62 percent approval rate for Pope Paul VI. Support for the cardinal's performance is lower among Catholics than the average rating among Americans for any president in the last forty years. It is exactly the same level as the approval given Richard Nixon in 1973, the year before his resignation—though it is 16 percentage points higher than the approval of Mr. Nixon on the average in 1974, the year he did resign. Nor can the cardinal's relatively low level of popularity be seen as a problem that all American bishops face, because in a national survey of American Catholics, 72 percent approved the way "the bishops" were handling their job.

The absence of enthusiasm for Cardinal Cody seems evenly distributed in the population. There is no significant difference in Cardinal Cody's popularity rating between young and old people, those in favor of church reform and those against it, men and women, college educated and non-college educated, those supporting racial integration and those opposing it. Among Irish Catholics, support for the cardinal goes to 48 percent, and among black Catholics, to 50 percent. Approval of his performance is lowest among Polish and Italian Catholics, with 39 percent of the former and 34 percent of the latter approving the way he is handling his job.

Active disapproval for the cardinal is strongest among devout Catholics. Forty percent of the weekly mass attenders disapprove of his job performance, as do 36 percent of those who pray every day and 38 percent of those who belong to parish organizations.

The cardinal's difficulties, then, seem to be widespread in the diocese and not to be the result of stands on specific religious or ecclesiastical or political issues. Nor is the reaction to him unimportant in terms of people's decisions about the Catholic Church. Thirty-seven percent of the respondents said that they were farther away from the Church now than they were ten years ago, and one-quarter of these—the largest proportion—gave as their reason disillusionment with diocesan or parochial authority.

Pope Paul VI fares much better than Cardinal Cody, with a 62 percent approval rating (the same as a national survey of Catholics recorded in 1974). While the approval rating for the pope is below that for parish priests and the average for Presidents Kennedy, Eisenhower, and Roosevelt, it is substantially above the approval rating of Americans for Presidents Truman, Nixon, and Ford. Nevertheless, only two-fifths of the Catholics in Chicago think that it is certainly true that "Jesus handed over the leadership of his Church to Peter and the popes." Only one-third think it is "certainly true" that the pope is infallible when he speaks on matters of faith and morals—virtually the same proportions reported in a 1974 national study of American Catholics (see Table A).

Immediately after they were asked to express their approval or disapproval of the way the pope "is handling his job," the interviewees 'were asked, "In 1968, Pope Paul forbade Catholics to use any method of artificial birth control. Do you agree or disagree with this position?" Even though 62 percent had said in the previous question that they in general approved of the way

155

Crisis in the Church

TABLE A

POPULARITY RATING OF CIVIL AND RELIGIOUS LEADERS
(per cent)

Question: "Do you approve or disapprove of the way ... is handling his job?"

	Chicago - 1977	National - 1974
Priests in your parish	84	82
President Kennedy (average for years in office)		76
Bishops*		72
The mayor in your town*	68	
President Roosevelt (average)		68
President Eisenhower (average)		66
Pope Paul*	62	62
President Nixon (average)		48
President Ford (average)		46
President Truman (average)		46
President Nixon (1973)		42
Cardinal Cody*	42	
President Nixon (1974**)		26

*Catholics only

**The year of his resignation

the pope was handling his job, only 18 percent said they agreed with the 1968 birth control decision. The Catholics of Chicago, then, clearly distinguish between a generalized approval for the pope and acceptance of specific papal teachings.

Catholics over 45 were more likely than those under 45 to accept the papal decision, but even within this older group, only 27 percent said they agreed with it. Similarly, Irish Catholics were somewhat more likely than members of other ethnic groups to agree with the pope on birth control, but only 22 percent of them expressed such agreement. There was no difference between men and women in the acceptance of the papal decision and no difference between those who had gone to college and those who had not done so. In other words, despite the decisiveness of the 1968 encyclical and the public support for the encyclical among the American hierarchy, more than four-fifths of the Catholics in the Archdiocese of Chicago categorically reject it.

Parish priests received the highest approval rating of any church leaders with more than four-fifths of the Catholics in Chicago (84 percent) approving the way "parish priests" are doing their jobs. But this generalized approval of the performance of parish priests coexists with rather low ratings of professional competence. Only one-fifth of the Catholics in Chicago consider their priests' sermons to be "excellent"—the same as the national average in a 1974 study. (In 1952, two-fifths, or 40 percent, of the Catholics in the country described sermons as "excellent.") Forty percent said that the priests in their parish were "very understanding" of the practical problems of their parishioners, and 35 percent said they were "very understanding" of the problems of teenagers. In both these matters the approval of Chicagoans for their clergy was beneath that of the national rating of priests three years ago. Forty-eight percent of the national sample said that priests were very understanding of practical problems and 47 percent said they were very understanding of teenagers. By narrow margins Chicago Catholics rejected the assertions that priests expect laity to be followers and that priests are not as religious as they used to be (40 percent agreed with the first statement, 48 percent with the second statement). But 26 percent of the Catholics in Cook and Lake counties agreed that "priests are unconcerned about people, only themselves"—9 percentage points above the 1974 national average.

Catholics under thirty are the most critical of sermons in the parish. Only 15 percent of them say that they are excellent. Even among Catholics over 45, however, the highest approval for sermons is given only by 25 percent. Nor is the criticism of sermons based on the greater educational achievement of Chicago Catholics (42 percent of them have attended college). College edu-

Crisis in the Church

cated Catholics are no less critical and no more critical of the sermons they hear on Sunday. Of the various ethnic groups in Chicago, 35 percent of the black Catholics, 26 percent of the Polish Catholics, and 22 percent of the Irish Catholics think that sermons are "excellent." Only 15 percent of the German Catholics give the same rating.

There is no significant difference between men and women in rating the competency of priests in understanding human problems, though Catholics over 45 are much more likely to say priests are very understanding (48 percent versus 34 percent). There is again no statistically significant relationship between the amount of education and the rating of the counseling skills of the clergy.

While Chicagoans give their parish priests a high general rating, they are less enthusiastic about both their sermons and their counseling skills. They are more likely than Catholics nationally to be critical of the professional competencies of their clergy and of their selfishness. Such criticisms of the clergy are related to age but are not related to educational achievement. In other words, whatever the failures of the clergy in the Archdiocese of Chicago, they do not seem to be the result of the increased educational attainment of their congregations.

Furthermore, only the minority of Catholics in the Chicago archdiocese are willing to concede the Church's right to teach what they should believe on racial integration (37 percent), birth control (29 percent), and abortion (48 percent). Three years ago, in a national study of Catholics, 54 percent agreed that the Church had the right to teach what stance Catholics should take on abortion. The majority of Chicago Catholics, in other words, do not accept the right of the Church to lay down binding teachings for them on birth control, abortion, or racial integration. Men are more likely than women (54 percent as opposed to 44 percent) to agree with the Church's right to teach on abortion, and people under 45 (45 percent) are less likely than those over 45 (55 percent) to accept the Church's right to lay down definitive teaching on abortion. Again, there are no

statistically significant differences related to educational achievement. The independence of Catholics on the abortion issue, as on
the birth control issue, is not a result of greater educational
attainment.

In summary, the authority crisis for Catholics in the Archdiocese of Chicago is severe—even more severe, it would seem,
than in other places of the American Catholic Church. The
cardinal archbishop is not popular, especially with the most devout Catholics and with those both on the right and the left
ecclesiastically and politically. The pope is respected, but the
overwhelming majority of Catholics reject his birth control
teaching. Parish priests are even more respected but are given
even lower ratings of professional competence than priests receive elsewhere in the country. The majority of Chicago Catholics reject the Church's right to lay down binding regulations
on birth control, abortion, and racial integration. There is no
evidence at all in the survey to indicate that any of these problems of authority are related to the higher educational achievement of Catholics in the years since the second World War. Even
though 42 percent of Cook and Lake County Catholics have
attended college, there are virtually no differences between college educated and others on any of the authority issues. Greater
independence is *not* the result of higher education.

By large majorities Roman Catholics in the Archdiocese of
Chicago (Cook and Lake counties) reject most of the official
teaching of the Catholic church on sexuality and abortion even
though only 7 percent of the women say that they personally
would seek an abortion for themselves for an unwanted child.
This turning away from the official teaching of the Church has
taken place in all ethnic, educational, and age groups, though it
is especially pronounced among Catholics under thirty.

Only 16 percent of Chicago Catholics disagreed with the
statement, "A married couple who feel they have as many children as they want are really not doing anything wrong when
they use artificial means to prevent conception." Only 26 percent reject the assertion that "Two people who are in love do not

do anything wrong when they marry even though one of them is divorced." And 48 percent reject the statement that "It is not really wrong for engaged couples to have some sexual relations before they are married." Three-quarters of the Catholics in the Archdiocese of Chicago are willing to think that "It should be possible for a pregnant woman to obtain a legal abortion if there is a strong chance of a serious birth defect in the baby." Thirty-four percent also agree that it should be legally possible to obtain an abortion if "she is married and does not want any more children." On the other hand, only 7 percent of the women said that they would definitely have an abortion if there was a serious reason for not having another child, and only 8 percent of the men said they would definitely want their wives to consider having an abortion. Another 20 percent, however, admitted that they "would consider" having an abortion.

Age is the strongest factor to predict the decline of acceptance of Catholic sexual morality. Eighty-four percent of the people over 45 think that premarital sex is wrong, and only 20 percent of those under 30 agree with them. One-quarter of those over 45 agree with the legalization of abortion for those who do not want any more children, while 40 percent of those under 30 support such legalized abortion. There is no statistically significant difference between men and women and between those who have attended college and those who have not (at least when age is held constant) in either support for the legalization of abortion or approval of premarital sex. Nor are there any significant differences among the various ethnic groups which make up the Archdiocese of Chicago.

Most Chicago Catholics seem to be good political pluralists. They would not have an abortion themselves (70 percent reject such a possibility—both men and women); on the other hand, they do not wish to make abortions illegal in the case of a defective child for those whose moral principles do not stand in the way. A substantial proportion of them (less than a majority, however) are in favor of a legalization of abortion which makes it little more than a form of contraception. There is no difference between Catholic women over 45 and those under 30 in the proportion saying they would definitely have an abortion (7 percent in both cases), though the women under 30 are much more likely (32 percent versus 10 percent) to say that they "would consider" having an abortion. The younger Catholic women, in other words, are not so willing to reject out of hand the possibility of an abortion.

A decade-and-a-half ago the majority of American Catholics accepted the Church's ban on birth control, premarital sex, and marriage after divorce. Since the early 1960s, approval of premarital sex has gone up dramatically, and the majority of Catholics approve of both birth control and divorce and in some circumstances even legalized abortion. There is virtually no difference between Catholics in the Archdiocese of Chicago on these matters and Catholics in the rest of the country. The Catholic Church's credibility as a teacher on sexual morality seems close to rock bottom both locally and nationally.

Devotion

While there is a crisis of credibility among Catholics in the Archdiocese of Chicago, there is no apparent crisis of faith. They are still more devout and better read than Catholics in the rest of America, and they are not inclined to leave the Church either because of the crisis of nonapproval of the Church's sexual teaching or the crisis of authority. While 15 percent of those who were born Catholic have left the Church, this loss has been more than made up for by converts to Roman Catholicism.

A little more than half (52 percent) of the Catholics in Cook and Lake counties go to church every Sunday; only 13 percent never go to church. Exactly one-third of the Catholics in the two counties receive Holy Communion every week (substantially more than the 24 percent who are weekly communicants nationally). Although only 15 percent go to confession weekly and 35 percent "almost never" go to confession, three-fifths of the Catholics in the Archdiocese of Chicago pray every day and four-fifths pray at least once a week.

Chicago Catholics are also much more likely to have attended

Crisis in the Church

a retreat in the last two years than are Catholics elsewhere (17 percent versus 4 percent) and to have made a Day of Recollection (35 percent versus 9 percent). They are also substantially more likely to have participated in a liturgy in someone's home (21 percent versus 8 percent), to have attended a charismatic prayer meeting (12 percent versus 6 percent), to have had a serious religious discussion with the priest (29 percent versus 20 percent), and to have participated in a religious discussion group (27 percent versus 20 percent). Despite the elaborate Catholic television network in Chicago, Catholics in the archdiocese are significantly less likely than Catholics nationally to have seen a Catholic radio or TV program in the last two years (30 percent in Chicago, 39 percent nationally). They are also less likely to have read a Catholic magazine or newspaper (42 percent versus 56 percent). On the other hand, Chicago Catholics are far more likely to have read a spiritual book during the last two years (55 percent versus 33 percent) and to belong to a parish organization (27 percent versus 18 percent). Finally, four-fifths of the Catholics in the archdiocese were married by a priest and four-fifths are married to other Catholics. Thus, a very high level of religious devotion and activity has been sustained among Catholics in the Archdiocese of Chicago despite the crisis of leadership which apparently exists in Chicago and the crisis of sexual credibility which seems to exist among all American Catholics.

Women are significantly more likely to go to mass weekly than men (58 percent versus 47 percent), and they are also more likely to receive communion weekly (39 percent versus 27 percent). Similarly, there are sharp differences in weekly mass attendance among age groups. Seventy-one percent of those over 45 go to church at least once a week, as do 43 percent of those between 30 and 45; only 38 percent of those under 35 go to church at least once a week. There is, however, a "u-curve" in the reception of Holy Communion. Both the older and the younger are more likely to receive communion every week than those in the middle years—37 percent for those over 45, 24 percent for those under 30, and 19 percent for those between 30 and 45. Sixty-three percent of those under thirty who go to church every week also receive Holy Communion every week. There is no statistical difference in church attendance among educational groups. The college educated are every bit as likely to attend church as those who had no college education. Again, this suggests that whatever the crisis may be among Chicago Catholics, it is not related to educational attainment.

There are very great differences, however, among the various ethnic groups. Sixty-eight percent of the Irish attend church weekly, 59 percent of the Polish, 48 percent of the Germans, 35 percent of the Italians, 48 percent of the blacks, and 39 percent of Latinos. Similar differences exist in the weekly reception of Holy Communion. Half the Irish in the archdiocese receive communion every week, but no other group goes above 35 percent (35 percent for the Germans, 26 percent for the Poles, 20 percent for the Italians, 29 percent for the blacks, and 20 percent for the Latinos).

Those over 45 are more likely to pray every day (75 percent) than those in the middle years (55 percent) or those under 30 (43 percent). However, there is no difference among those who pray at least once a week. Once again, there is no significant relationship between educational attainment and frequency of prayer, although black Catholics are the most likely to report daily prayer (76 percent), followed by Latino Catholics (73 percent), Irish Catholics (64 percent), Polish Catholics (58 percent), German Catholics (54 percent), and Italian Catholics (53 percent).

A slight majority of Catholics, then, are in church every Sunday, a third of them receive Holy Communion every week, and almost four-fifths pray every week. Even the young people, who are less devout in their church attendance, still pray in overwhelming numbers at least once a week. There is no evidence at all of a link between educational attainment and religious devotion, so it cannot be the case that as Catholics become better informed they become less devout. Chicago Catholics are also

Crisis in the Church

much more likely than Catholics in other parts of the country to engage in retreats, Days of Recollection, home liturgies, discussion groups, pentecostal prayer meetings, and to read spiritual books. The crisis of leadership and credibility in the Roman Catholic Archdiocese of Chicago cannot be seen as a crisis of the dissolution of the Catholic Church.

Contributions

Despite the crisis of sexual credibility which seems to affect the whole American Catholic church and the acute leadership crisis which seems to be special to the church in the Archdiocese of Chicago, Roman Catholics in Cook and Lake counties are still substantially more generous in their annual contributions to the Church than are American Catholics nationally. They are also quite willing to contribute more money for the support of their parishes within the archdiocese. Catholic families in Cook and Lake counties gave $279 on the average to their church last year, which was approximately 2 percent of their annual income. In 1974, a national study of American Catholics showed that they gave $180 annually to the Church, which was only 1.6 percent of the annual family income of the typical American Catholic. The Irish and the Germans are the most generous of Chicago Catholics, both giving approximately $324 a year of family income to the Church (1.8 percent of the Irish income and 2.48 percent of the German income). Poles give on the average $214 a year, Italians $256, Latinos $183, and blacks $275—for black Catholics an extraordinarily high 3.8 percent of their family income (perhaps a manifestation of the enthusiastic black support for inner-city Catholic schools).

Both older and younger people are somewhat more generous in their contributions than those between thirty and forty-five. Those over forty-five give 2.5 percent of their income to the Church, those under thirty give 1.6 percent, those between thirty and forty-five give 1.4 percent. However, each of these phases of the life cycle has different sets of financial demands, so it may well be that the proportion of income available for church contribution will vary at different stages of the life cycle. Similarly, the college educated and those who did not graduate from high school are more generous than the high school graduates. Those who have less than a high school education give 2.1 percent of their income, those with a college education give 2.3 percent, and the high school graduates who did not attend college give 1.6 percent of their income (still more than the national average for Roman Catholics).

Assuming that Catholics are 35 percent of the population of Cook County (a valid assumption based on a number of different surveys), there are 600,000 Catholic families and unrelated individuals in Cook County. Thus the total contribution of Catholics to the Church in the Archdiocese of Chicago in the previous year can be estimated at $167.4 million—somewhat higher than the approximately $150 million reported by the Chicago chancery office, but still not an unreasonable estimate given the fact that Catholics contribute to other religious activities besides their parish and the strong possibility that many pastors keep separate record books (the chancery office may not receive an accurate report of parish contributions in many cases).

Furthermore, the generosity of Chicago Catholics has not yet been fully challenged. The respondents to the survey were asked, "If there were a collection every year to help the Catholic schools in very poor parishes in the inner city, do you think your family would contribute? Seventy percent of the Catholics in the sample said they would contribute to such a collection, and the mean amount mentioned was $33.95.

If 420,000 Catholic families and unrelated individuals did make this extra contribution to help schools in the poor parishes, some $14.6 million would be added to the diocesan resources available to deal with the inner city school situation. If such collections were carried on in every parish, there would be some $18 million a year more available for Catholic education.

There are no differences either by age or education in the proportion of increase of contribution such a collection would

165

produce. For all age and education groups, it is one-half of one percent of annual family income. Irish Catholics in the archdiocese would be the heaviest contributors with $107 per family (six-tenths of one percent of their annual family income), German Catholics would contribute $98 more a year, Polish Catholics $73 more a year, and Italian Catholics $62 more a year (six-tenths of one percent of the income of the Germans and the Italians, and four-tenths of one percent of the income of the Poles). There are, incidentally, no statistically significant differences among the various ethnic groups in Chicago in the proportion saying they would be willing to contribute to such a special collection, though the Irish are more likely than the rest of the groups (78 percent) to say they would contribute.

Thus despite the twin crises of leadership and sexuality, Catholics in the Archdiocese of Chicago not only have remained loyal to the Church, they continue to be generous contributors—more generous than Catholics elsewhere—and indeed willing to increase notably their generosity for the service of the predominantly black schools in inner-city parishes.

Clergy

Despite the recent decision by the Congregation of the Faith in Rome that it would be impossible to ordain women priests in the Catholic Church, two-fifths of the Catholics in the Archdiocese of Chicago support the ordination of women. In 1974, in a national study of American Catholics, only 29 percent supported the ordination of women. However, surveys done by the Gallup organization since the decision in early February by the Congregation of the Faith (speaking for Paul VI) show that in the wake of that decision there has been a dramatic increase in the support for the ordination of women. Among the total American Catholic population there is no difference at all between the support for ordination of women nationally and the support among Catholics in the Archdiocese of Chicago. The distribution of responses to the women as priests question suggests that it is a rising issue: Agree Strongly 22%, Agree Somewhat 18%, Disagree Somewhat 11%, Disagree Strongly 40%. It is thus the extreme positions—strong agreement, strong disagreement—that receive the highest proportions of support.

The support for the ordination of women is especially strong among young Catholics. Twenty-two percent of those over forty-five would agree with the ordination of women. Thirty-six percent of those between thirty and forty-five and 48 percent of those under thirty think that it would be good to ordain women priests. Interestingly enough, men are more likely to support women priests than women—44 percent of the men and only 34 percent of the women support the change. Also, the college educated (47 percent) are much more likely than noncollege educated (34 percent) to agree with the idea of women priests.

The relationship between age and sex and the ordination of women is interesting.

PROPORTION MEN AND WOMEN SUPPORTING
ORDINATION OF WOMEN

Age	Men	Women
Over 45	28%	18%
30-45	52	32
Under 30	53	63

Majority support for the ordination of women can be found among all men under 45, and there is little difference between those over 30 and those under 30. On the other hand, 20 percentage points fewer women in the age bracket between 30 and 45 support the ordination of women than do men—only 32 percent of the women in the middle years would support the ordination of women. There is a big leap of 31 percentage points, however, when one comes to women under 30 who are not only immensely more likely than older women to support ordination of women, they are also the only ones in any age group who are more likely than men of the same age to support ordination of women. The impact of feminism on the younger generation of Catholic women is clear from the table above.

Crisis in the Church

There is, however, majority support among Catholics for married men priests. Three-quarters of the Catholics in Cook and Lake counties say they could accept such a change, and 56 percent positively would approve such a change. The leadership of the Archdiocese of Chicago, therefore, finds itself on the one hand with documents from Rome denying the possibility of the ordination of women and refusing to change the discipline of the Western Church against married priests, while on the other hand it has majority support among its membership for a married clergy and majority support among men under 45 and among women under 30 for the ordination of women. It is an awkward position for any leadership group.

Catholics are still positive about the possibility of a priest or nun in their families. About half reject the notion that they would be unhappy if a daughter became a nun, and 62 percent say they would be "very pleased" if a son of theirs should choose to be a priest (the same as the national average for a daughter's becoming a nun and 12 percentage points higher than the national average of the 1974 study for a son's becoming a priest). At the present time in Chicago, two-thirds say they would be "very pleased" if their son should choose to be a business executive. Thus, for Chicago Catholics, there is a somewhat higher approval of a business career for a son than for the priesthood. Women would be more pleased than men to have a son become a priest (59 percent versus 49 percent); among those under thirty, the proportion falls to 47 percent, as opposed to 63 percent among those over forty-five. There is no significant difference among education groups in enthusiasm for a priestly vocation in their family, nor are there any statistically significant differences among ethnic groups.

So the priesthood is still a respected profession, but not as respected as that of business executive. Only the future will tell whether there will be married priests and women priests and whether such changes will heighten the enthusiasm of parents for having a son (or daughter) in the Catholic priesthood.

Andrew Greeley

Changes in the Church

The crisis in Catholicism in the Archdiocese of Chicago at the present time is not the result of dissatisfaction with changes in the Church which have occurred since the Second Vatican Council. Only one-fifth of the Catholics in the archdiocese (the same proportion as the national average in 1974) are opposed to the changes. Sixty-nine percent approve of guitar masses, 80 percent are in favor of the "handshake of peace" ceremony midway through the mass, 62 percent approve nuns wearing ordinary clothes instead of special religious habits, 68 percent approve new ways of teaching religion in the schools, and half are in favor of distribution of communion by lay people at mass. Despite the fierce controversy that has raged in some Chicago parishes on the subject, only 16 percent of Catholics in the archdiocese are opposed to sex education being taught in Catholic schools.

The strongest opposition to the changes in the Church come from those over forty-five. Still, only 31 percent of them are opposed to the changes (17 percent of those between 30 and 45, and 12 percent of those under 30). Similarly, the strongest opposition to sex education in Catholic schools comes from those over forty-five, though only 29 percent of that age category are opposed to sex education, as are 10 percent of those in the middle years and 5 percent of those under 30. The strongest opposition to sex education in the Catholic schools comes from those who have less than a high school diploma—22 percent as opposed to 12 percent of those who graduated from high school and only 5 percent of those who graduated from college. The greatest opposition to the changes in the Church since the Vatican Council comes from those who have graduated from high school—28 percent oppose the changes in this educational group compared with 23 percent of those who did not graduate from high school and 14 percent of the college educated Catholics who are opposed to such changes.

Crisis in the Church

By way of summary, Chicago Catholics are anything but ecclesiastical conservatives. As we have seen, they feel free to be
critical of their leadership and to choose which Catholic teaching
they will accept seriously. A majority of them support a married
clergy, and a majority of the men under 45 and the women under
30 support a female clergy. They enthusiastically applaud the
changes that have happened since the Vatican Council and are
opposed neither to new methods of religious education nor sex
education in Catholic schools. Even among those population
groups where there is more opposition to the changes, it is still
a very small minority that stands opposed. Whatever may be said
of some of its leadership, the rank and file Catholics in the
Archdiocese of Chicago seem to like their new Church.

Race and Anti-Semitism

While they are progressive on ecclesiastical matters, Chicago
Catholics present a mixed picture on attitudes toward minority
groups in American society. They are even lower on measures of
anti-Semitism than the national Catholic average, but the majority are uneasy about neighborhood integration. Still, 64 percent of their elementary school children and 75 percent of their
high school children (91 percent if they are in Catholic high
schools) are in integrated schools.

Two standard items have been used for many years to measure
anti-Semitic attitudes and were used in this survey of Catholics
in Lake and Cook counties: "Jewish businessmen are about as
honest as other businessmen" and "Jews have too much power
in the United States." On the first question, 21 percent gave an
anti-Semitic answer; on the second, 29 percent. These proportions do not differ from those reported in other large cities in the
country. Two comments can be made about these figures. On
the one hand, the majority of Catholics do not give anti-Semitic
responses; on the other hand, enough of a minority do to make
Jews uneasy and to alert Catholic religious leaders that the problem of anti-Semitism has not been eliminated both in the Church

and in American society. (Other research shows that Catholics are less anti-Semitic than Protestants and may be less anti-Semitic than Jews are anti-Catholic.) The lowest anti-Semitism rate is among Irish and German Catholics, 21 percent of whom agree that Jews have too much power in the United States. The highest rate is among Polish and Italian Catholics, 35 percent of whom think Jews have too much power. Unlike most other variables in this research, attitudes against Jews do relate to education. Forty-three percent of those who did not graduate from high school think that Jews have too much power as opposed to 25 percent of those who attended college. However, education and time will not eliminate the problem of the residual anti-Semitism among certain Catholics, because there is no correlation between youthfulness and positive attitudes toward Jews.

It would doubtless be appropriate for Jewish and Catholic agencies to combine to study attitudes of the members of each group toward the other.

The two racial items used in the study were "Blacks shouldn't push themselves where they're not wanted" and "White people have a right to live in an all-white neighborhood if they want to and blacks should respect that right." Thirty-eight percent of Chicago Catholics reject the first statement and only 26 percent reject the second. In the first statement Chicago Catholics are no different from other Catholics in the United States and in the second they are not different from those living in large cities where threatened neighborhoods are common. Eighty-two percent of Chicago Catholics say they would not object to a school in which a few students were black; 55 percent say they would not object to a school where half the students were black, and one-third say they would not object to a school where most of the students were black—approximately the same responses as were obtained from other Catholic respondents in large cities throughout the country. The willingness of Catholics to send their children to schools where at least a few students are black is confirmed by the fact that 64 percent of the parents with children in elementary schools in Cook and Lake counties say that there are blacks in the schools their children attend—with no difference between those in Catholic schools and those in public schools. Eighty percent of those with children in high school say they are in integrated high schools (90 percent of the Catholic high schools, 80 percent of the public schools).

The Irish, the Germans, and the Italians are more likely than Poles to reject the idea of the right of whites to keep the neighborhoods that way. Thirty-four percent of the Germans, 31 percent of the Irish, 30 percent of the Italians, and fifteen percent of the Poles reject it. But even in the more moderate groups, more than two-thirds agree that whites have the right to keep their neighborhoods the way they are. Similarly, 35 percent of those under 30 (as opposed to 21 percent of those over 60) and 38 percent of those who attended college reject the right of whites to keep neighborhoods the way they are. But more than 60 percent of both groups would defend that right. Neighborhoods, then, are clearly a critical point in the Archdiocese of Chicago. More than half the Latinos accept the right of white people to keep neighborhoods the way they are.

It should be observed that national survey data indicate that even in big cities of the north, Catholics are more prointegration than Protestants, though somewhat less so than Jews. (There are only slight differences between Irish Catholics and Jews in their attitudes toward integration.) Nevertheless, there is plenty of evidence in the Chicago data that racial and religious tensions persist in Cook and Lake counties.

The majority of Chicago Catholics, then, accept in both theory and practice some kind of school integration, and a majority are not anti-Semitic. But there is strong resistance to neighborhood integration and a strong residue of anti-Semitism, particularly in certain ethnic groups. However, since virtually all Catholic schools are neighborhood schools, it would follow that whatever their attitudes might be toward protecting neighborhoods, some 60 percent of Chicago Catholics with school age children do in fact live in racially integrated neighborhoods.

Schools

Only 9 percent of Catholics in the Archdiocese of Chicago think there is no more need for Catholic schools. Forty percent of the elementary school children of Chicago Catholics are in parochial schools (as opposed to 29 percent nationally), as are 37 percent of the high school students and 33 percent of the college students whose parents live in Cook and Lake counties. Seventy-five percent of Chicago's Catholics are satisfied with the religious education in Catholic schools (not significantly different from that reported in a national Catholic sample studied in 1974), although only 55 percent (opposed to 72 percent nationally) are satisfied with the secular education children are receiving in Catholic schools. The principal advantages of Catholic schools seen by parents are religious education (half the respondents) and the emphasis on obedience and discipline (36 percent).

Despite the changes in Catholic schools, Catholic enthusiasm for them has continued high. Two-thirds approve the new methods of religious instruction, three-quarters approve of sex education in Catholic schools, and two-thirds think lay teachers can do as good a job as nuns do. Three-quarters of Chicago Catholics support federal aid to Catholic schools and two-fifths think that Catholic schools would get federal support were it not for anti-Catholic feeling in the government. More than half the Catholics in the Archdiocese of Chicago think they have an obligation to continue to support the schools even if they have no children in them.

There have been few Catholic schools constructed in the Archdiocese of Chicago in the last ten years, and many inner-city schools have closed. Yet Chicago Catholics show a considerable willingness to increase their contributions to keep inner-city schools open.* There is a similar willingness to support existing

---

* Seventy percent of the Catholics in the Chicago sample said they would contribute to a collection every year to help the Catholic schools in very poor parishes in the inner city. The mean amount mentioned was $33, a one-quarter increase in their annual contributions to the Church.

Crisis in the Church

Catholic schools in the respondents' own parishes. The respondents were asked, "Suppose you were in a parish which had an elementary school which had been in existence for as long as you could remember and had done a good job of educating children. The pastor announced one Sunday that the school would have to close because of financial problems unless everyone in the parish gave extra money to support it. Would you be willing to donate some more money to keep the school going—that is, more than you give now?" Seventy-five percent said they would be willing, 20 percent said they would not, and 5 percent said they did not know. The average contribution per year of those who said they would be willing to contribute was $39.25.

Only 8 percent of the respondents said there were no Catholic schools in their parishes. While such a number is too small for one to base confident estimates upon, it seems that a little less than half the parishioners in such parishes would support school construction, and about the same proportion would send their children to such schools if they were constructed—about the same proportion as do in fact have children in Catholic schools in other parishes. There is, therefore, a clear difference among Catholics in their willingness to keep open an existing school and their willingness to construct a new one, although a substantial proportion seem willing even to support the construction of new schools.

Catholics in Chicago, then, despite problems of leadership and sexuality, still strongly support the parochial school system regardless of age or educational achievement. They are willing to make major financial contributions both to keep inner-city schools open and to maintain their own parochial school. There is more difference of opinion—though here the numbers are too small for any confidence—on the construction of new schools.

Young People in Chicago

On balance, then, Chicago does not seem to be in worse shape than the rest of the American Church; if anything, Catholics in

Chicago are more devout and generous. They give more money, are more likely to receive communion every week, are more willing to support a priestly vocation in their family. Despite the unpopularity of the cardinal and dissatisfaction with some aspects of clerical service and leadership, the crisis among Chicago Catholics seems marginally less serious than it is in the rest of the country.

But are Catholics under thirty in Chicago seriously affected by the diocesan crisis of leadership? Table 1 suggests that they are not. Indeed, they are twice as likely to receive communion as are their youthful counterparts in the rest of the country. Twenty-eight percent of Catholics under thirty receive communion every week, as do 13 percent of the Catholics under thirty nationally and 31 percent of those over thirty. Young Chicago Catholics, then, are almost as likely to receive weekly communion as are older Catholics nationally. Furthermore, only one-third of Catholics under thirty receive communion once a year or less, as opposed to half the Catholics under thirty nationally. They are somewhat less likely to pray every day (11 percentage points), but 12 percentage points more likely to say they would be pleased if a son became a priest. Chicago Catholics under thirty are also even more sympathetic toward premarital sex among engaged couples and remarriage after divorce than their national counterparts. Three-fifths of them support the ordination of women, as opposed to two-fifths of the young Catholics nationally.

The unpopularity of the archbishop, then, does not seem to have had an important negative effect on the religious devotion and loyalty of youthful Catholics in the Archdiocese of Chicago.

Change Among Chicago Catholics

It might be argued, however, that in fact there has been a serious harmful effect of the unpopular archdiocesan administration. Catholics in Chicago may be slightly more devout than the rest of the country at the present time, but in the past it may have

175

Crisis in the Church

TABLE 1

ATTITUDES OF CATHOLICS UNDER 30 IN CHICAGO

(Per cent)

	Chicago	U.S.
Weekly church attendance	37	37
Church less than once a month	41	40
Communion weekly	28	13
Communion once a year or less	33	49
Prayer once a day	41	52
Prayer at least once a week	72	81
Very pleased with a son choosing the priesthood	55	43
Sermons are excellent	15	12
Priest expect laity to be followers	43	41
Approve premarital sex among engaged couples	38	73
Approve remarriage after divorce	96	82
Approve birth control	89	92
Church has the right to teach what Catholics should believe about abortion	44	45
Pope is infallible when he speaks as head of the Church (certainly true)	21	22
Support ordination of women	60	39
Pope is head of church as successor to Peter (certainly true)	31	34

been that they were much more devout. So there may have been an even more serious decline in Chicago than there has been in the rest of the nation. The unpopularity of the archbishop may have contributed to that decline. The data in Table 2, however, suggest that this is not the case. Support for the doctrinal and ethical teaching was no higher in Chicago in 1963 than it was

176

in the rest of the country. The changes in these items, while statistically significant, are no larger than they were nationally. The decline in weekly mass attendance has been less precipitous in Chicago, because in 1963 Chicago Catholics were somewhat less

TABLE 2

CHANGES AMONG CHICAGO CATHOLICS, 1963–1976

	1963 (n=110)	1976 (n=619)
Devotion		
Weekly mass attendance	65%	53%*
Less than monthly mass attendance	24	26
Weekly communion	13	32**
Communion yearly or less	32	32
Daily private prayer	73	57*
Monthly confession	24	12*
Read a spiritual book in the last year	67	55*
Doctrine		
Average number of children per family	2.44	2.08*
Premarital sex among engaged wrong	82%	45%*
Divorce wrong	39	21*
Birth control wrong	50	15*
Pope successor to Peter and head of Church (% certain)	75	47
Intergroup Relations		
Blacks shouldn't push (% disagree)	24	35**
Whites have right to keep neighborhood white	17	26**
Jews as honest as any other businesmen	80	70*
Jews have too much power (% disagree)	83	60
Vocation		
Would be pleased if son became a priest (% strongly)	58	62
Would be pleased if daughter became a nun (% strongly)	53	52

*Decline is statistically significant.

**Increase is statistically significant.

177

likely than the rest of the country to attend weekly mass. The increase in weekly communion in the years since 1963 has been especially dramatic in Chicago. Nationally, communion reception went up from 12 to 24 percent; in Chicago it went up from 13 to 32 percent. Only in the decline in private prayer—15 percentage points in Chicago and 14 percentage points nationally—does there seem to be a moderate additional Chicago decline. Finally, there has been no significant change at all between 1963 and 1976 in support for religious vocations in the family among Chicago Catholics.*

So whatever is to be said about the popularity and effectiveness of the archdiocesan administration, it does not seem to have had an additional negative impact on Catholic religious behavior. Indeed, in the years since 1963, Catholic attitudes toward racial integration have improved significantly, even though there has been an inexplicable decline in their attitudes toward Jews (though the majority of Catholics reject both the anti-Semitic items in Table 2).

My colleagues and I developed for *Catholic Schools in a Declining Church* a five-variable, d-systems model which accounted for most of the change in Catholic religious devotion between 1963 and 1974. The principal intervening variables (Figure 1) between time and religious devotion are cohort (the influx of a younger generation), papal authority (the increase in the proportion questioning that the pope is the successor of Peter as head of the Church), and birth control (the increased proportion

---

* The NORC 1963 study of Catholic schools had a much larger sample than the 1974 study—more than 2,000 respondents. Since Chicagoans are about 5 percent of the population in the country, it was possible to draw out of the 1963 sample 110 Chicago Catholics. Obviously, comparisons between 110 respondents and 609 respondents leave something to be desired. Nonetheless, strict tests of statistical significance were used in preparing this section of the analysis. The hypothesis that the decline in Chicago has been more precipitous than in the rest of the country simply does not stand up in the face of the data.

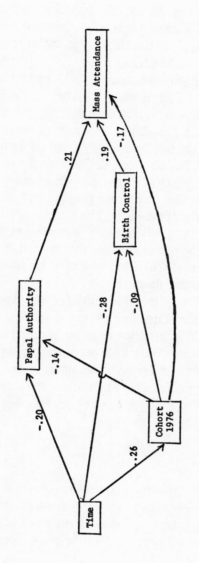

Figure 1.—Social Change Model

179

Crisis in the Church

rejecting the Church's official birth control teaching.* It seems logical to reason that if a similar model can also account for a decline in devotion among Chicago Catholics, then there is no additional influence on the decline to be attributed to the unpopularity of the archbishop.

In fact the similarity between Table 3 and Table 5.9 (p. 128, *Catholic Schools . . .*) is quite striking. Both locally and nationally, the d-systems model accounts for all of the change in mass attendance and in daily prayer. It accounts nationally for 86 percent of the decline in monthly confession, and, in Chicago, for 83 percent of the decline. Nationally, the sexual ethic issue accounted for 46 percent of the decline in mass attendance, 38 percent of the decline in private prayer, and 55 percent of the decline in monthly confession. The figures for Chicago are respectively 47 percent, 40 percent, and 58 percent. Try as one might (and I tried), one cannot attribute the deterioration in religious behavior of Chicago lay Catholics to the unpopularity of the cardinal archbishop.

Table 3 also shows that four-fifths of the decline in spiritual reading can be accounted for by the d-systems model. Both in 1963 and in 1976, Catholics read far more than their national counterparts; but there was a 12 percentage point decline among Chicagoans. A little more than two-fifths of that decline can be accounted for by doctrinal shifts, and a little more than one-fifth is attributable to a younger age cohort less disposed to reading spiritual material.

Conclusion

Chicago Catholics give their archbishop low ratings on job performance. They are also more critical of their clergy on some matters than are other Catholics. Nonetheless, the Archdiocese of Chicago seems to have ridden out the Catholic storm of the

---

* For a detailed explanation of this model, see Chapter 5 in *Catholic Schools in a Declining Church.*

TABLE 3

EXPLANATION OF CHICAGO CATHOLIC RELIGIOUS DECLINE
ACCORDING TO SOCIAL CHANGE MODEL

	Mass	Private Prayer	Confession	Reading a spiritual book
Percentage point decline	13	16	12	16
Proportion of decline attributable to birth control value change	.47	.40	.58	.29
Proportion attributable to papal authority change	.16	.44	.17	.14
Proportion attributable to new cohort	.13	.16	.08	.36
Proportion unexplained by the model	.00	.00	.17	.21
TOTAL	1.00	1.00	1.00	1.00

last decade-and-a-half with somewhat more vigor and strength than the rest of the American Church. Speculation as to why this might be the case is beyond the scope of this book. In the short run, therefore, it would appear that the perceived failings of clergy and hierarchy have little effect on the behavior of the ordinary Catholic laity. Indeed, in Chicago, Catholicism has fared better than it has in the rest of the country since 1963, despite such failures.

Chapter Eight

THE SECULARIZATION ISSUE:
OBSTACLE TO EVANGELIZATION?

IN attempting to discuss the "secularization" model of religious change, one is faced with the problem that rarely do those who speak so glibly about secularization bother to define what they mean. One has the impression that social theorists are so superior that they need not waste their time with such trivia as defining terms. Thus when the empiricist tries to define the term and then operationalize it into measures, the theorist airily dismisses the empiricist's work, saying that isn't what he means at all. Take, for example, the following comments from three sociologists at the University of Notre Dame:

> . . . this [ecumenical] movement parallels the fundamental tendency of industrial societies, compared to more primitive types of societies, to drift away from supernaturalism toward a more rational-technical world-view. We do not mean to imply that Catholics and other bureaucratized denominations are abandoning religion in favor of (Weberian) rationality, but rather that their members are increasingly discarding mystical precepts.[1]

Leaving aside the fact that the serious students of industrializing societies in the third world—such as Alex Inkeles and Lloyd and Suzanne Rudolph—take a much more sophisticated and

183

skeptical view of this "fundamental tendency" (in fact they deny its existence), one would dearly like to know what the "mystical precepts" are which are being abandoned so that one could test the assertion against empirical data. But like cold "theoreticians," they play their cards close to the vest and don't tell you what they mean. Later in their paper they comment:

A theoretically-oriented sociologist is, then, prompted to wonder what part the encyclical [*Humanae Vitae*] explanation of declining church attendance played in relation to larger events occurring in American society during and immediately preceding the 1968-1972 period. This was the time of Father Groppi's marches through Milwaukee, some of the most painful years of the Vietnam conflict, years characterized by student unrest, political assassinations, ghetto and barrio uprisings, and "white flight"—both Catholic and Protestants—from the inner cities. Catholic acceptance of traditional theological doctrine declined over the decade as much as acceptance of Church teachings on sex and divorce. These global disruptions and changes of the late 1960s may well have had a disillusioning effect and other effects upon Catholics at least equal to the effects of the encyclical.[2]

Such generalizations represent either a very high level of wisdom or a banality that scarcely deserves the name of social science. Note well that there is no way the impact of Father Groppi's marches on the religious behavior of Catholics can be measured, no way the impact of the Vietnam war can be measured. These assertions about secularization are beyond proof or disproof. They are oracular, pontifical, solemn; they are also unverifiable. The Notre Dame scholars are "sophisticated" social theorists, which apparently means they can say anything they please without defining their terms or advancing evidence to sustain their assertions. They may be taken as either wise men or fools but not social scientists.

Still, some of us must strive to define what is meant by "secularization" and attempt to find evidence either for it or against it in empirical data.* For the purposes of this chapter, and at the risk of being dismissed as a naive empiricist, I will define secularization as a decline in religious enthusiasm, belief, and activity—a decline brought on by the higher level of religious sophistication of ordinary people. The way to measure such decline is through time-series measures: that is, by comparing data collected at one or several times in the past with data collected more recently. The secularization explanation would hypothesize that if one has data at time A and time A + 1 and time A + 2 on any given measure of religious behavior, there will be a decline.

In the absence of time-series data, we can make the assumption that younger people and better educated people represent the leading edge of the evolutionary process of secularization. If the secularization dynamic is at work in the society, it will work most effectively among the most sophisticated members of the society; it will be most obvious among the younger members of society who are further down the line in the evolutionary development than their predecessors.

In this chapter we will consider three measures of religious behavior, the importance of which few observers of religious behavior would challenge: prayer, religious experience, and belief in life after death. We will see whether either the time-series model or the age-and-education model demonstrates any decline in the frequency of prayer, the proportion believing in life after death, and in the prevalence of mystical experiences, particularly the "twice born" experiences of the sort described by William James in his classic book, *The Varieties of Religious Experience*.

---

* This issue is discussed at great length in my *Unsecular Man* (New York: Schocken, 1972) and also, in somewhat less length and with more acrimony, in my paper for the Catholic Theological Society meetings in Toronto, June 1-3, 1977, "Sociology and Theology: Some Methodological Questions."

Crisis in the Church

Prayer

Fifty-four percent of the American people (Table 1) pray every day, half of that number (27 percent) pray several times a day. Only one-quarter of the population prays less than once a week, and only 4 percent of Americans do not pray at all.

TABLE 1

FREQUENCY OF PRAYER
(Per cent)

Never	4
Less than once a week	22
Once a week	7
Several times a week	13
Once a day	27
Several times a day	27

Baptists, "Other" Protestant denominations (for the most part fundamentalists), and nondenominational Protestants pray the most, with almost two-fifths of each group praying several times a day (Table 2). Jews pray the least: only 13 percent of them pray daily, 58 percent pray less than once a week, and 10 percent do not pray at all. However, even among those who have no religion, a quarter pray at least once a week.

TABLE 2

FREQUENCY OF PRAYER BY DENOMINATION
(Per cent)

Denomination	Never	Less than 1 a week	1 a week	Several times week	1 a day	Several times day	Total
Baptist	2	16	6	13	26	38	291
Methodist	3	21	7	10	32	27	183
Presbyterian	1	25	6	18	29	21	80
Episcopalian	6	17	17	6	31	23	35
Lutheran	-	20	11	23	26	21	101
"Other" Protestant	3	14	6	10	27	39	175
No denomination Protestant	4	30	2	7	16	41	44
Roman Catholic	.8	19	10	15	33	23	368
Jewish	10	58	6	13	10	3	31
No religion	29	46	2	9	10	4	99
"Other" religion	3	29	3	17	20	29	35

N = 1442

Women are much more likely to pray than men. Sixty-five percent of the women pray every day, while only 43 percent of the men pray daily; 37 percent of the men pray less than once a week, as opposed to 15 percent of the women (Table 3A). Those who pray least frequently are young people between twenty and twenty-nine: 37 percent of them pray every day. Still, 65 percent of the people in the country between twenty and twenty-nine pray at least once a week. Older people are more likely to pray than younger people; whether that is a part of the life cycle, location, or historical trend cannot be determined from the existing data.

TABLE 3A

FREQUENCY OF PRAYER BY SEX OF RESPONDENT
(Per cent)

	Never	Less than 1 a week	1 a week	Several times a week	1 a day	Several times a day	Total
Male	6	31	9	12	22	20	672
Female	2	14	6	14	31	34	775

N = 1447

TABLE 3B

FREQUENCY OF PRAYER BY AGE OF RESPONDENT
(Per cent)

	Never	Less than 1 a week	1 a week	Several times a week	1 a day	Several times a day	Total
20-29	5	30	10	18	22	15	356
30-39	4	26	8	17	24	21	259
40-49	3	20	6	11	28	32	244
50-59	2	17	5	10	29	36	237
60-69	2	10	5	10	37	36	169
70 +	2	13	6	6	32	42	126

N = 1447

One might think that prayer is an especially Southern phenomenon because of the presence in the South of the intense pieties of Southern Baptist and fundamentalist denominations. It is true (Table 4) that daily prayer is most frequent in the South (58 percent), but the "pagan" Northeast is only 2 percentage points behind, and the North Central region only 4 more points behind the South. It is in the West (the Rocky Mountain and Pacific Coast States) that one finds less than a majority praying every day (but still, 48 percent of those in the western region of the country pray daily).

TABLE 4

FREQUENCY OF PRAYER BY REGION
(Per cent daily)

Northeast	56
North Central	52
South	58
West	48

N = 1447

The gamma association between daily prayer and psychological well-being, as measured by a scale developed by Professor Norman Bradburn of the University of Chicago and National Opinion Research Center, is .34, and the association between daily prayer and marital adjustment is .26. Both associations are highly significant statistically, and are among the highest measures of association ever found in the indices of Professor Bradburn. Prayer, it turns out, is good for you.

In previous research, it was reported that a .4 association was found between frequent mystical experiences and the Bradburn psychological well-being index. However, only 5 percent of the American population have had frequent mystical experiences, and half the American population prays every day. In terms of psychological well-being, in other words, daily prayer seems to be a useful substitute for mystical ecstasy.

Attempts to explain the relationship between frequent prayer and psychological well-being and marriage adjustment were unsuccessful. The relationship could not be accounted for by hopefulness, a feeling of closeness to God, conviction in life after death, region, denomination, mystical experience, or the conviction that God is love. We can only say, then, that frequent prayer does indeed seem to make people happier; we cannot offer an explanation for this relationship.* The present analysis enables us only to sketch out the fact of widespread prayer and its association with psychological well-being. We do not know how Americans pray, why they pray, when they pray, to whom they pray, or what they pray; and we cannot even explain why prayer seems to make them happier.

College-education (Table 5) does not make Americans any less likely to pray. Fifty-four percent of Americans under thirty pray several times a week or more whether they attend college or not. College attenders over thirty are four percentage points less likely to pray than those over thirty who did not go to college, but that difference is not statistically significant. However, those over thirty are significantly more likely to pray than those under thirty (in the national population, though not, as we have seen in an earlier chapter, among Roman Catholics, where there is no statistical difference—except in Chicago—in the frequency of

---

* Among the various denominations, the correlation between psychological well-being and devotion was statistically significant for the Baptists, the Presbyterians, the "other" and nondenominational Protestants, and Roman Catholics. It was not, however, significant for Methodists, Episcopalians, Lutherans and Jews. The relationship was also statistically significant in the West, the South and North Central, but not in the Northeastern region of the country.

prayer between those under thirty and those over thirty). There is, then, some support for the secularization hypothesis in Table 5. Education does not lead to a decline of prayer, but young people are less likely to pray than older people, though one cannot say whether this is a result of their age or of some long-term trend which will lead to a decline in prayer. The secularization hypothesis is surely not confirmed by Table 5, but there is some evidence in its favor—though not particularly powerful evidence when one considers that the majority of people under thirty still pray several times a week.

TABLE 5

PRAY SEVERAL TIMES A WEEK OR MORE BY EDUCATION BY AGE
(Per cent)

Education	Under 30	Over 30
No college	54 (235)	71* (754)
College	54 (176)	67* (280)

*Significantly different from "under 30." No significant relationships with education.

Unfortunately, the question asked in the NORC 1973 Basic Belief Study (on which Tables 1-5 are based) was never asked previously, so no time-series data are available to enable us to determine precisely whether young people pray more often as they get older. However, two questions were asked in the Ben Gaffin-Gallup studies for the *Catholic Digest*[3] of 1953 and 1965. The wording of the questions was sufficiently different that direct comparisons between the NORC studies and the *Catholic Digest* studies are risky, but it would appear that there are more respondents who did not pray at all in 1953 and 1965 than there were in 1973—8 percent of the respondents said they did not pray in the *Catholic Digest* study, and only 4 percent in the NORC study (Table 6). In all three projects, those under thirty who said they never prayed were 1 percentage point higher than the national average—giving some support to the hypothesis that young people pray more often as they grow older. Table 6 surely provides no evidence that there has been an increase since 1953 in the proportion of Americans—young or older—who never pray. One should be wary of arguing that there is a decline in the proportion that never pray because of the different wording of the questionnaire items, but there is no support for the notion that the non-praying proportion has increased in the American population in the last quarter century. At least nine-tenths of the American public prayed in 1953, and at least nine-tenths of them still pray.

TABLE 6

PROPORTION "NEVER PRAY"

	All Respondents
1953[*]	8%
1965[*]	8%
1973[**]	4%
	Under 30
1953[*]	9%
1965[*]	9%
1973[**]	5%

[*] "How many times did you pray in the last seven days?" Response: "Do not pray."

[**] "How often do you pray?" Response: "Never."

Andrew Greeley

*Life after Death and Religious Experience**

In preparing this section I collected survey data on attitudes toward death from a number of major countries at various periods in time. The principal hypothesis to be tested from the secularization theory contends that in advanced industrial society, educated, sophisticated human beings cannot take religious myths seriously. The more industrialized the society and the more recent the survey indicator, it would be argued, the lower will be the proportion of the population which believes in life after death.

The data summarized in Table 7 are necessarily ambiguous. The surveys were taken at different times in different countries with sampling frames of varying quality and in the context of different surveys with question wordings that may not convey quite the same nuances in one language they do in another. Furthermore, it is quite possible that even if the accurate nuances were captured, there would be political and social implications to belief in life after death that would differ from country to country. Thus in one country it may be difficult to be a member of the left wing and concede belief in doctrine that has been used by the right wing to oppress or control the working class. One would have to get at deep-seated religious convictions under such circumstances through a rather different kind of question.

With all these reservations, Table 7 still provides fascinating though complex information. If one concedes that the United States is the most advanced and most sophisticated industrial society in the world and that the American people have the highest educational attainment, then there is no confirmation for the secularization hypothesis in Table 7. Belief in life after death has remained at a high level in the United States between 1936 and 1973, with some fluctuations but with a net gain of 3 percentage points in those asserting belief in survival.

---

* An earlier form of this section appeared in the international journal *Concilium*.

TABLE 7

INTERNATIONAL DATA ON BELIEF IN LIFE AFTER DEATH

(Per Cent Believing)

	1936	1939	1944	1945	1947	1948	1958	1960	1961	1964	1968	1973-77
U.S.A.	64	--	76	--	68	68	--	74	74	--	73	70
Canada	--	--	--	84	78	--	--	--	68	--	--	--
England . . .	--	49	--	--	49	--	--	--	56	--	38	--
Czechoslovakia	--	--	--	38	--	--	--	--	--	--	--	--
Brazil	--	--	--	--	78	--	48	--	--	--	--	--
Norway	--	--	--	--	71	--	66	--	71	--	54	--
Finland . . .	--	--	--	--	69	--	--	--	--	--	55	--
Holland . . .	--	--	--	--	68	--	--	--	63	--	50	--
Australia . .	--	--	--	--	63	--	--	--	--	--	--	--
France	--	--	--	--	58	--	--	--	57	--	--	--
Denmark . . .	--	--	--	--	59	--	--	--	--	--	--	--
Sweden	--	--	--	--	49	--	--	--	--	--	38	--
Greece	--	--	--	--	--	--	--	--	--	--	58	--
West Germany .	--	--	--	--	--	--	47	--	38	38	42	--
Switzerland .	--	--	--	--	--	--	--	--	55	--	--	--
Japan	--	--	--	--	--	--	30	--	--	--	--	--

For other countries the picture is more ambiguous. There is, generally speaking, no major downswing between 1947 and 1961, save in Brazil (in a survey apparently limited to cities); but in the short seven years between 1961 and 1968, there were dramatic declines in England, Norway, and Holland, and a moderate increase in West Germany.

Even in 1968, however, in only three of the countries for which data were available—England, Sweden, and West Germany—do less than half the population believe in life after death. In contrast, in 1958, only 30 percent of the Japanese believed in it.

It is difficult to say what the reason for the decline between 1961 and 1968 was. It was a period of unparalleled prosperity in Europe; perhaps the abundance of goods led to a weakening of religious faith, or perhaps there was a change in the wording of the questions put to the respondents.* In Germany, for example, the "don't know" response was replaced with an "impossible to say," which, it seems reasonable to assume, notably changed the options available to the respondents.

There are fascinating historical, sociological and religious questions that arise from Table 7. Why, for example, are citizens of one of the two great English-speaking democracies twice as likely to believe in life after death as are the citizens of the other? If we grant that there has been no modification of question wording in the last fifteen years, why has there been a general decline in Western European countries in secularization, where presumably it should be the farthest advanced? Such variations in the North Atlantic cultural community, which has so much in common in so many ways, suggest that intensive research ought to be done not merely on religious beliefs in these various countries but in the context of their basic belief systems. The Catholic Church should not be uninterested in such research.

---

* Within the time limitations imposed in the preparation of this book, there was no way to determine the exact wording of the questions asked in the various questionnaires.

Crisis in the Church

The secularization hypothesis would also suggest that it is precisely among the young and better educated that evolution away from religious superstition ought to be most evident. Cross tabulations by sex, denomination, age, and education were available for three countries. They are presented in Tables 8 to 11. In all three countries, the United States, Germany, and England, women are more likely to believe in life after death than men, though the differences in the United States (6 percentage points in 1973) were less than half as great as the differences in the two European countries.

TABLE 8

BELIEF IN LIFE AFTER DEATH BY SEX

(Per Cent)

Country and Year	Male	Female
United States		
1944	73	79
1960	68	78
1973	67	73
Germany		
1964	31	44
England		
1968	32	46

Protestants, Catholics, and "others"* are most likely to believe in human survival in the U. S. In Germany, Catholics are more

---

* The "other" category in survey research represents approximately 3 percent of the population. It includes such diverse groups as Ukranian Orthodox Catholics who refuse to be categorized as "Roman," Anglo-Catholics who reject the terminology "Protestant," and fundamentalist denominations eager to distinguish themselves from mainland Protestants, as well as Mormons, orientals, and other small groups.

likely to believe in survival than Protestants. Obviously, these two denominational affiliations mean something very different in the two countries, although the proportion of American Catholics who believe in life after death in the 1973 NORC study seems surprisingly small. (Checked against two other NORC studies, however, the data in Table 9 seem to stand.)

TABLE 9

BELIEF IN LIFE AFTER DEATH BY DENOMINATION

(Per Cent)

Country and Year	Protestant	Catholic	Jew	None	Other
United States					
1973	71	70	31	33	73
Germany					
1964	30	49	--	--	31

Finally Tables 10 and 11 test the secularization hypothesis. Are the young and the better educated less likely than other population groups to believe in life after death? In the United States and in Germany the relationship is curved, with those of intermediate education the most likely to believe in survival. But the differences are very small—4 points in the U.S. and 6-7 points in Germany. The secularization hypothesis is *not* sustained in Table 10. The better educated are not inclined to be skeptical.

Furthermore, while the very old are slightly more likely than others to believe in human survival (Table 11), there is no linear relationship between age and belief in life after death. The differences between the youngest age category and those in their sixties in the United States is 7 percentage points, in Germany 5 percentage points, and in England 2 percentage points. Thus there is no reason to believe that in these three countries rising

levels of education or the moving of new age cohorts through
the life cycle will lead to a notable decline in belief in life after
death. The secularization hypothesis.is *not* sustained by Table 11.

TABLE 10

BELIEF IN LIFE AFTER DEATH BY EDUCATIONAL ATTAINMENT

(Per Cent)

Country and Year	Primary	Secondary	Higher
United States 1973	68	72	70
Germany 1964	37	44	38

TABLE 11

BELIEF IN LIFE AFTER DEATH BY AGE

(Per Cent)

Age	United States 1973	Germany 1964	England 1968
20 - 29	69	34	37
30 - 39	69	37 (30-44 yrs. old)	35
40 - 49	69		41
50 - 59	69	39 (45-69 yrs. old)	35
60 - 69	73	46 Over 60)	41 (65 and over)
Over 70	76		

In the United States there is absolutely no evidence that secularization has led to a decline in belief of life after death. The time-series data show that some 70 percent of Americans have believed in human survival since the 1930s. Moreover (Table 12), there is no relationship between education and age and belief in life after death. Thus those under thirty who have graduate school education are just as likely as those over forty-five with no college at all to believe in human survival—70 percent in both cases, which is exactly the national average. Those with no college under forty-five and those between thirty and forty-five who attended graduate school believe somewhat less than the national average; but there is no consistent pattern, no evidence of evolutionary change, and no significant correlations between either age or education on the one hand and belief in life after death on the other. The secularization assumptions to the contrary, conviction about human survival has not changed in the United States in the last forty years, and there is no reason, on the basis of considering the young and the better educated, to think that it will change for the next forty years.

TABLE 12

PER CENT BELIEVE IN LIFE AFTER DEATH BY AGE BY EDUCATION
(NORC General Social Survey—1972-1977)

	18-29	30-45	Over 45	Average
No college	$64_{(680)}$	$66_{(837)}$	$70_{(1583)}$	69
College	$70_{(536)}$	$73_{(331)}$	$71_{(369)}$	72
Graduate school	$70_{(56)}$	$64_{(102)}$	$74_{(68)}$	66
Average	$67_{(1172)}$	$72_{(1270)}$	$70_{(2020)}$	70

Crisis in the Church

A more dramatic question than belief in life after death is actual contact with the dead. As far as we know, this question has been asked in only one survey, the Basic Belief study conducted in the United States by NORC in 1973. A surprisingly high number of Americans—25 percent—report they have been "really" in contact with the dead.*

TABLE 13

DEMOGRAPHIC BACKGROUND OF THOSE WHO HAVE CONTACT WITH THE DEAD
(Per Cent in U.S.A.)

	Age			Sex			Race	
	Ever	Fre-quent-ly		Ever	Fre-quent-ly		Ever	Fre-quent-ly
Teens	31	0	Male	23	3	White	24	3
20's	23	2						
30's	21	2	Female	34	4	Black	46	5
40's	27	4						
50's	34	3						
60's	40	4						
Over 70	39	9						

---

* We were badly handicapped by the fact that we were unable to ask our respondents any more than whether they had such experiences. It would be important to know whether the experiences were dreaming or awake, whether there was conversation with the dead person, what the circumstances were at the time of contact, whether anyone else was present, whether the dead person was actually seen or his presence sensed, whether the respondent felt that it was an extraordinary "supernatural" event or merely a strange feeling one might have upon visiting the grave of a departed friend or relative. Also, how did the 25 percent reporting such contact interpret the adverb "really"?

Who were the people who had such experiences? As one might expect, such experiences were more frequent with the old. Two-fifths of those over sixty reported such experiences, and 9 percent of those over seventy reported them frequently (Table 13). But 31 percent of the teenagers reported such experiences, which makes them more likely to report them than those in their twenties, thirties, or forties. Older people are most likely to have experienced bereavement, so perhaps they are more likely to *want* contact with the dead. The relatively high score among teenagers is harder to explain—perhaps they are more psychically sensitive or simply more interested in bizarre events and more likely to want to experience them.

Women are more likely than men to have had contact with the dead. Blacks are much more likely to report it than whites, with 46 percent of the black population having had at least one such experience and 23 percent having it frequently or sometimes.

Table 14 shows that of the three major religious affiliations, Jews are more likely to report contact with the dead (even though Jewish belief in an afterlife is not nearly so strong as the Christian belief), and Protestants are more likely to report it than Catholics. But even though 18 percent of those who have no religion at all report some contact with the dead, two-fifths of those whose religion is "other" claim such contact. Among the Protestant denominations, the Episcopalians are most likely to have had a contact with the dead experience, followed by the "other" Protestants (mostly fundamentalist denominations) and then by the Methodists. Forty-four percent of the Episcopalian respondents report at least one contact with the dead, as have 32 percent of the Methodists. The relatively low Roman Catholic score may be the result of the fact that Catholics are more likely to believe in human survival and have less need of such experiences—though as we shall see later, belief in survival correlates quite positively with contact with the dead. Among the Catholic ethnic groups, the Poles and the Spanish-speaking (34 percent) are those who most frequently report a contact with the dead experience. The Germans are the least likely among both

TABLE 14

CONTACT WITH THE DEAD EXPERIENCES FY RELIGIOUS AFFILIATION, PROTESTANT DENOMINATION, AND RELIGIO-ETHNICITY

(Per Cent in U.S.A. Ever)

Affiliation	Per Cent	Protestant Denomination	Per Cent	Religio-Ethnicity	Per Cent
Protestant(899)	30	Baptist(282)	30	Protestant	
Catholic(361)	26	Methodist(181)	32	British(167)	30
Jew(29)	32	Lutheran(101)	28	German(131)	24
Other(98)	40	Presbyterian(74)	27	Scandinavian(47)	21
None(46)	18	Episcopalian(35)	44	Irish(72)	31
		Other(173)	35	American(87)	24
		No denomination(40)	67	Catholic	
				Irish(47)	25
				German(48)	15
				Italian(52)	30
				Polish(43)	34
				Spanish-Speaking(33)	34
				Jew(28)	33

Protestants and Catholics to report such experiences. One colleague suggested to me that the high incidence of contact with the dead among the Poles and Jews is the result of the fact that in both groups there is a very strong tie with parents, a tie which may facilitate the conviction that a deceased parent has not completely ended his existence at death.

Contact with the dead correlates negatively with education and income (Table 15). Those who have had such experiences are less likely to have been to college and less likely to earn over $10,000 than are those who have not had such experiences.

TABLE 15

CONTACT WITH THE DEAD EXPERIENCES BY EDUCATION AND INCOME
(Per Cent)

Frequency of Experience	College	$10,000 or more
Never	35	50
Once or twice	25	48
Several times	27	38
Often	23	22

Is there any relationship between marital status and contact with the dead? Are those who have lost a spouse likely to have such experiences? It is obvious that they are (Table 16). Half of those who have lost a spouse report "real" contact with the dead, and 12 percent report such contact "often." To look at the matter the other way around, 21 percent of those who have had contact with the dead are widows or widowers, and 28 percent who have had frequent contact with the dead are widows or widowers; but this group is only 7 percent of the population.

Crisis in the Church

TABLE 16

CONTACT WITH THE DEAD EXPERIENCES BY MARITAL STATUS
(Per Cent in U.S.A.)

Marital Status	Never	Frequency Once or Twice	Several Times	Often
Married (1053)	74	16	7	3
Widowed (110)*	49	18	21	12
Divorced (64)	63	27	8	3
Separated (32)	66	22	13	0
Never Married	73	16	8	2

*Twenty-one per cent of the sample who had contact with the dead "several times" and 28 per cent of the sample reporting it "often" are widowed. They are only 7 per cent of the general population.

It could also be argued that if somehow the barrier that separates the living from the dead can be penetrated, it would most likely be accomplished precisely by those who are still united in a powerful bond of love. Who else, in other words, would be expected to maintain contact after death? Besides, the correlation is a correlation, not a total explanation. The majority of those who have contact with the dead are *not* widows or widowers; he who writes off contact with the dead as wish fulfillment is as dogmatic as he who thinks that such experiences are proof of human survival. All social science can say is that older people, women, and widows and widowers are more likely to report such experiences than anyone else. Those who have such experiences do not seem to be all that much different from the rest of the population in other respects.

But they are less well educated. Does it not follow that those who are better educated and more sophisticated are less likely to fall victim to such superstitious nonsense? The question is a fair one, but it must be noted that given the change of educational levels of achievement in the United States over the last half century, older people are much less likely to have graduated from high school and to have gone to college. Thus the question becomes, does the lower level of educational achievement relate directly to contact with the dead experience or is it merely a spurious relationship resulting from the fact that older people are less well educated?

Figure 1 indicates decisively that the latter is the case. In the three-variable model there is no correlation between attending college and contact with the dead. Being over forty relates both negatively to college attendance and positively to contact with the dead, and the relationship between attending college and not having such experiences "often" or "several times" turns out to be spurious.

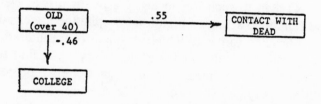

Figure 1--Relationship between Age and Education with Contact with the Dead Experiences "Often" or "Several Times."

What does it mean to say that more than half the people in the North Atlantic community believe in life after death and that one-quarter of the people in the United States report having had actual contact with the dead? Does this represent a decline from some previous age of faith, or does it rather indicate continuity with the past? Unfortunately, there is no good way to answer the question. Any attempt to postulate higher levels of belief in survival for any earlier era of Western history must necessarily be extremely speculative. We do not know how citizens of the thirteenth, the fifteenth, seventeenth, or ninth centuries would respond to questions from a Gallup or an NORC interview. But it is naive to think that atheism, agnosticism, skepticism, and doubt are twentieth-century discoveries. We know, of course, that there have been "Godless" districts in England and France for hundreds of years. French researchers suggest that "missions" in certain districts many hundreds of years ago have shaped the religiousness of those districts ever since. Similarly, revivalistic movements in England in the seventeenth and eighteenth centuries seem to account for the considerable diversity in religious practice in different sections of the English countryside. It is not unreasonable to assume that there never was a time in human history when belief in survival was easy.

So it is inappropriate to ask why the conviction of human survival has fallen to such low levels. We might just as well ask why it has remained at such a high level despite the attacks of the various secularizing forces to which so much of the literature of sociology of religion is devoted. Instead of trying to find trends where there are no base lines, it would seem better to be content to ask why so many people believe in life after death.

Humans believe in life after death because there is a powerful unconscious drive in their personalities toward that conviction. Freud said that the unconscious believes itself to be immortal. Dream researchers report an unshakable conviction of immortality revealed in dreams.

A yearning for immortality is built into the very structure of the human personality. We can make a rational decision that this yearning is self-deceptive and should be rejected, but such a decision may not convince the unconscious. Those who responded that they believe in life after death in our surveys are following the thrust of the unconscious; those who say they do not believe are rejecting the yearnings of the unconscious. To say this does not imply that either group of respondents is right; it is merely to assert that he who denies human survival gives a negative answer to one of the deepest yearnings of his own personality.[4]

How deep the yearning for immortality is emerges from the small but growing field of "sudden death" research. Scholars interested in this discipline interview people who have experienced certain-death situations and yet have survived. (A parachute fails to open and the chutist survives, a mountaineer falls 500 feet down the face of a mountain, a wheel falls off a speeding car, for example.) There seems to be a regular pattern in such experiences. First, the person is very angry at whoever is responsible for his predicament. Then his life passes before him in review; resignation takes possession of him, which is followed by a feeling of peace and serenity. Finally, in what seem to be the last moments of life, the serenity is replaced by an overwhelming hope and, at the last instant, something very like mystical ecstasy.*

A description of this precise process may be found in an old essay by G. K. Chesterton in which he describes an accident on a London street in a hansom cab when the horse went out of control. Admitting that he was once skeptical of those who claimed to see the whole of life pass by in a moment when threatened by death, Chesterton wrote:

> But in those few moments, while my cab was tearing toward the traffic of the Strand, I discovered that there is a truth behind this phrase, as there is behind all popular phrases. I really did have, in that short and shrieking period, a rapid succession of a number of fundamental points of view. I had, so to speak, about five religions in almost as many seconds. My first religion was pure Paganism, which among sincere men is more shortly described as extreme fear. Then there succeeded a

---

* In our national sample survey research on mystical experience, William McCready and I have discovered that even in the general population, death experiences can trigger ecstasy.

state of mind which is quite real, but for which no proper name has ever been found. The ancients called it Stoicism, and I think it must be what some German lunatics mean (if they mean anything) when they talk about Pessimism. It was an empty and open acceptance of the thing that happens—as if one had got beyond the value of it. And then, curiously enough, came a very strong contrary feeling—that things mattered very much indeed, and yet that they were something more than tragic. It was a feeling, not that life was unimportant, but that life was much too important ever to be anything but life. I hope that this was Christianity. At any rate, it occurred at the moment when we went crash into the omnibus.[5]

One cannot claim, of course, that such experiences (and they are, incidentally, very different in their dynamics from those whose brush with death follows an illness of some duration) prove there is life after death. There seems no way this subject can be resolved scientifically. The dead have not testified that they survive, at least not in any way scientific research would deem acceptable. One might then assume that they do not survive; if they did, they would surely communicate with us in some less dubious fashion than what is reported by parapsychologists. Such an assumption is surely not unreasonable, but it is hardly a scientific conclusion. Science as such must file the question of life after death in a folder marked "unproven and probably unprovable." But in the folder there must go two notations: "There is no certain evidence of survival," and "There is a strong conviction in the depths of the human personality that survival does occur." Science must then close the file cabinet with an agnostic shrug of the shoulders.

Since we can neither validate nor invalidate our powerful inborn conviction of survival, we must do something about it. Is that deeply rooted conviction a revelation, a hint of an explanation, the best single evidence we have of a gracious universe? Or is it the final cruel self-deception of a cold, vicious, unfeeling universe? There is no way to escape the question, and no way one can avoid giving some sort of an answer, however tentative and however much it may depend on some sort of existential leap.

Does the hope and the ecstasy of the final moments of the sudden death experience represent merely a response of the species to the prospect of sudden and immediate oblivion? Is it merely an evolutionary adaptation, or is it a hint of something better to come?

Peter Berger, among others, has argued that in such experiences of hope, laughter, play, and love, humans intuit purposefulness in their lives. Doubtless they do, but the critical question is whether such an intuition may not be simply a form of wish fulfillment and self-deception. The pose of the skeptical scientist who writes it all off as emotional immaturity is not as tough and hardnosed as it might appear. He is making a trans-scientific (or, if one wishes, metaphysical) judgment—like the poet who sees entangled in the leaves of the tree "the Cheshire smile which sets us fearfully free." Both choices are hard to make, both are fearful, both provide a certain kind of freedom, and both require a substantial leap beyond the existing data.

It is undeniable that those who have had powerful mystical experiences have little doubt about survival. There is a strong positive correlation between frequent mystical experiences and the conviction that the human personality survives death. As one person who had two such experiences in his life put it to me, "Once you have been through one of those things, the question of survival almost becomes irrelevant. You know that Reality is good—very, very good—and it doesn't seem necessary to ask anything more." Interestingly enough, it is precisely among those mystics who score very high on measures of psychic health that the conviction of survival is strongest.*

---

* The correlation between the Psychological Well-Being scale and frequent mystical experience is .4—the highest existing correlation with that scale. For information on the scale itself, see Norman M. Bradburn, *The Structure of Psychological Well-Being,* Chicago: Aldine Press, 1969.

Crisis in the Church

Do these "mystical experiences," which correlate at .4 with psychological well-being, correlate with age and education? Are younger and better educated people less likely to think they have been in direct contact with the ultimate powers of the universe? In fact, it is precisely the college educated who are more likely to report having had such experiences—39 percent of those under thirty and 45 percent of those over thirty among the college attenders have had at least one such experience in their life. Older people are slightly more likely to report them than younger people (Table 17), but the difference is not statistically significant.

TABLE 17

MYSTICAL EXPERIENCES BY EDUCATION BY AGE
(Per Cent Ever)

	Under 30	Over 30
No college	28(235)	35(754)
Attended college	39*(176)	45*(280)

*Significantly higher than no college. Age differences are not statistically significant.

On the other hand, younger respondents are significantly likely to have a higher score on the "twice-born" scale (Table 18),* a scale which measures whether the ecstatic interlude

* A factor analysis of "descriptor" items shows a relationship among the following "descriptors": "A great increase in my understanding of knowledge," "A sense that I was bathed in light," "A feeling that I couldn't possibly describe what was happening to me," "The sensation of my personality having been taken over by something much more powerful than I am."

210

corresponds to that described by William James in his *Varieties of Religious Experiences* and Mircea Eliade in his essay on light.[6] Twenty-eight percent of those under thirty who have had such experiences had at least two of the twice-born phenomena, while only 21 percent over thirty had such experiences. Thus, if the kind of ecstasy described by William James is an indicator of religion, one is forced to say that far from being less religious than those over thirty, the younger people, at least those with intense experiences of the sacred, are more religious.

TABLE 18

PER CENT "HIGH"[a] ON "TWICE BORN" SCALE
BY AGE BY EDUCATION

	Under 30	Over 30
No college	23[*] (64)	21 (256)
Attended college	28[*] (67)	21 (125)

[a] Score 2 or more "twice born" phenomena.

[*] Younger respondents significantly more likely to be on "twice born" scale. No education effect.

Conclusion

The secularization model will not go away simply because it has not been supported. It has persisted for many years despite the fact that little empirical evidence for it has ever been found. However, those who are seriously interested in evangelization should be aware that they cannot dismiss airily the obstacles they encounter by attributing resistance to their efforts to "secularization" or "secularism." All the evidence indicates that belief in life after death, frequency of prayer, and the prevalence of

Crisis in the Church

religious experience, particularly twice-born experiences, are not diminishing in American society. Americans believe in survival, experience the sacred, and pray to the Ultimate at about the same rates they have in any past we can measure through survey data. The idea that the various crises in the 1960s in American life had a great impact on American religiousness—offered with such fervent conviction by the three Notre Dame sociologists that not one thought to adduce evidence to support it—simply is not supported by the data. Those whose concerns are with religious policy are engaging in self-deception if they choose to blame their problems on "secularism."

Chapter Nine

THE SEXUALITY ISSUE

THERE are three aspects of the sexuality issue that are pertinent to the questions being considered in this book:

(1) To what extent is the devotional and organizational crisis troubling the Roman Catholic Church at present the result of dissatisfaction with the Church's sexual teaching?

(2) Are the sexual changes going on in society today such that any evangelization effort on the part of the Catholic Church will begin with very serious obstacles to its success unless there is a "reformulation" of the Church's sexual ethic?

(3) If there is to be a "reformulation," can we find any hints in the existing empirical evidence to indicate the direction in which the Church might proceed? Is it possible to preserve the core of its own traditional wisdom and at the same time address itself to the poignant and powerful needs of contemporary humans?

To summarize briefly, by way of overview, the answers to these questions, sexuality is indeed part of contemporary Catholicism's problem, but certain highly specific sexual issues, most notably birth control, have created the problem, *not* a sweeping "sexual revolution." Secondly, given the changing attitudes towards sexual behavior in the United States and the resulting ambiguities, uncertainties, strains, and problems, a large number of Americans would not seriously listen to "Good News" preached by a church which lacks sexual credibility. Finally, there are some hints about possible reformulations of the Catholic sexual ethic, but they suggest that considerable careful research, balancing and hard work will be necessary if such a reformulation is to occur. Research, thought, and hard work are unfortunately the kinds of effort that many evangelization enthusiasts would like to escape.

There is a wide diversity in sexual attitudes among contemporary Americans. Only 22 percent of American Jews, for example, think that premarital sex is wrong, as opposed to 52 percent of the Baptists in the country (Table 1). Seventy-one percent of the Jews think that extramarital sex is wrong, as do 90 percent of the British Protestants. Thirty-eight percent of the Jewish respondents agree that homosexuality is always wrong, as opposed to 83 percent of the Baptists. Fifty-seven percent of the blacks and 48 percent of the Jews think that divorce laws ought to be made easier, as opposed to 18 percent of the Scandinavian Protestants and 17 percent of the German Catholics. One-quarter of the Jews and 27 percent of the blacks would support a law banning all pornography, but approximately half of the Slavic Catholics and the German Protestants would support such a law. Thirty-seven percent of the Jews and 34 percent of the Hispanics have seen an X-rated movie, while only 14 percent of the Episcopalians and 14 percent of the Scandinavian Protestants have slipped into darkened theaters to see what a pornographic film is like.

One the average, the majority of Americans still reject premarital sex and overwhelmingly reject extramarital sex and homosexuality. The majority are also against making divorce laws easier but also against banning all pornography. Only on the making of birth control information available to teenagers does there seem to be a virtual consensus, with 93 percent of the Jews, 78 percent of the Baptist and Irish Catholics, and 79 percent of the blacks approving the availability of birth control information for teenagers. On all the other six measures of the "sexual revolution," majority support does not exist in all groups for greater permissiveness.

TABLE 1

RANK ORDER OF ETHNIC GROUP AND DENOMINATIONS ON 7 SEXUALITY ITEMS
ON THE NORC GENERAL SOCIAL SURVEY

(Per Cent)

Premarital Sex Wrong (always/sometimes)		Extramarital Sex Wrong (always/sometimes)		Homosexuality Always Wrong		Birth Control Information to Teenagers Yes	
Jewish	22(15/7)	Jewish	71(48/23)	Jewish	38	Jewish	93
Episcopalian	32(16/16)	Black	76(64/12)	Episcopalian	50	Episcopalian	92
Black	34(26/18)	Presbyterian	76(59/17)	Irish Catholic	60	Presbyterian	87
Lutheran	37(22/15)	Episcopalian	78(56/22)	Presbyterian	66	Lutheran	85
Presbyterian	38(24/14)	Hispanic	81(74/7)	Italian Cath.	68	British Prot.	83
Methodist	39(35/14)	Scan. Prot.	82(7/15)	Slavic Cath.	70	German Prot.	81
Italian Cath.	40(29/11)	Italian Cath.	83(67/16)	Hispanic	73	Hispanic	82
Hispanic	42(32/10)	German Cath.	86(73/13)	German Cath.	74	Methodist	80
Slavic Cath.	43(35/8)	Irish Catholic	88(69/19)	Lutheran	75	German Cath.	80
Scan. Prot.	44(37/17)	Slavic Cath.	88(73/15)	German Prot.	77	Slavic Cath.	80
German Cath.	46(32/14)	German Prot.	89(69/20)	Scan. Prot.	77	Italian Cath.	80
Irish Catholic	47(32/15)	Baptist	89(78/11)	Black	77	Black	79
German Prot.	47(32/15)	Methodist	90(74/16)	Methodist	78	Irish Catholic	78
Baptist	52(41/11)	British Prot.	90(74/16)	Baptist	83	Baptist	78
ALL	46(33/13)	ALL	85(71/14)	ALL	72	ALL	83

215

TABLE 1 Continued .

Divorce Laws Should be Made Easier		Support Laws Banning Pornography		Have Seen an X-Rated Movie	
Black	57	Jewish	24	Jewish	37
Jewish	48	Black	27	Hispanic	34
Hispanic	36	Italian Catholic	38	Black	25
Episcopalian	35	Hispanic	38	Italian Catholic	25
Presbyterian	34	Episcopalian	41	Slavic Catholic	23
Baptist	34	German Catholic	41	German Catholic	21
Italian Catholic	34	Presbyterian	43	Irish Catholic	20
Lutheran	29	Irish Catholic	44	Methodist	18
British Protestant	27	Baptist	44	Presbyterian	18
Methodist	25	Scandinavian Protestant	44	Baptist	17
German Protestant	24	Lutheran	44	Lutheran	16
Irish Catholic	23	British Protestant	48	German Protestant	15
Slavic Catholic	22	Methodist	48	British Protestant	15
Scandinavian Protestant	18	Slavic Catholic	48	Episcopalian	14
German Catholic	17	German Protestant	50	Scandinavian Protestant	14

216

Interestingly enough, in most cases the Catholics are somewhere in the middle of the population between the Jews and the Baptists. Jews, Presbyterians, and Episcopalians tend to be the most "liberal" on matters of sexual permissiveness; blacks are "liberal" on premarital and extramarital sex, divorce, pornography, and X-rated movies but "conservative" on homosexuality. Italian and Hispanic Catholics tend to be generally at the more permissive end of the list of ethnic groups, while German and Slavic Catholics tend to be at the more "conservative" half of the list. As in so many other areas of human behavior, the Irish prove difficult to categorize. They are slightly more conservative than the national average on premarital and extramarital sex and in their attitudes toward divorce and pornography laws. On the other hand, the Irish Catholics are more likely than all Protestant groups in the country to have seen an X-rated movie (though slightly less likely than their Italian, Hispanic and Slavic counterparts). However, only Jews and Episcopalians are more tolerant on homosexuality than Irish Catholics. There is nothing in the Irish Catholic tradition, as far as this writer is aware, which would explain this relative tolerance of homosexuality. The Catholic Church, in its American manifestation, strongly influenced by the Irish tradition, has vigorously resisted any attempts to modify the Church's stern reaction to homosexual activity. On the other hand, the practice for many decades was that Irish-American clergy tended to be sympathetic in counseling homosexuals. (For this I have nothing more than my own impressions to cite as evidence.)

Catholics are not, however, among the most "conservative" groups in America on any issue but the easing of divorce laws, an issue in which three of the four most conservative groups are Catholic—Irish, Slavic, and German. On all other issues Methodists, Baptists, and German and British Protestants tend to be more "conservative" sexually than are Catholics. This despite the fact that in the Church's official sexual ethic, premarital and extramarital sex, homosexuality, birth control, divorce and pornography would certainly be condemned as seriously sinful. (X-rated movies would probably also be condemned.) Catholics, in other words, do not take the kinds of personal stands on sexual issues that one would expect of them considering the very conservative stand of the official Church on these matters.

Several of the Catholic groups, most especially the Irish, demonstrate a notable "liberalizing" trend among their younger members. Four of the sexual permissiveness items were combined into a scale (premarital sex, extramarital sex, homosexuality, and birth control information for teenagers). A Z-score (a percentage of a standard deviation above or below the mean) was computed for each of the groups (Table 2). Since the Jewish score is the most "liberal" in each of the three age categories, Table 2 consists of a comparison of each of the groups with the Jewish group. One can measure change in the direction of greater liberalism in a given group in comparison with change that is going on within the most liberal of the groups. Thus a —.49 for British Protestants in the oldest age category means that the British Protestants between 46 and 89 had a —.23 Z-score, or 49 points (about a half a standard deviation) beneath the Jews of comparable age. In the 46 to 89 year-old category, Irish Catholics are the most "conservative" in the country, being well over one standard deviation less permissive than Jews. In the 30 to 45 year-old category, the Irish Catholics are slightly more than a standard deviation more conservative on sexual matters than Jews. However, in the age group under 30, Irish Catholics and Slavic Catholics are only about a half a standard deviation more conservative than Jews, Irish Catholics being —.48 and Slavic Catholics —.41 Z-points more conservative than Jews. The 18-29 year-old category, in other words, for the two especially devout groups, Slavs and Irish, are second only to Jews in their permissiveness, having passed the Italians, who in the two previous age groups were the most sexually permissive of the Catholic ethnic communities.

Among the oldest group, the Italians were the most liberal of the Catholics on sexual matters. They change relatively little across age categories. Germans continue to be conservative in

TABLE 2

DIFFERENCE FROM JEWISH SCORE ON SEXUAL PERMISSIVENESS SCALE BY AGE BY ETHNIC GROUP*

(Z Scores)

	Age		
	46-89	30-45	18-29
(Jewish Score)	(.26)	(1.03)	(1.16)
British Protestant	-.49	.99	-.79
Scandinavian Protestant	-.56	.93	-.68
Slavic Catholic	-.56	.75	-.41
German Protestant	-.63	-1.03	-1.01
German Catholic	-.64	-1.15	-1.01
Italian Catholic	-.65	-.65	-.59
Black	-.74	-.71	-.68
Hispanic	-.74	-1.06	-.61
Irish Catholic	-.89	-1.05	-.48

*Groups ranked according to 46-89 ordering.

all three categories, as do Hispanics. The Slavs were relatively liberal in the oldest age group and become even more so in the youngest group. For the Irish the change has been from being the most conservative on sexual matters among those over 30 to being third most "liberal" (preceded by the Slavs and the Jews) of those under 30.

A number of observations are in order about Tables 1 and 2.

(1) There are a number of different sexual subcultures within the American Catholic community—Italians, relatively liberal; German, relatively conservative; Slavs and Irish, quite unpredictable.

(2) On most matters, however, Catholics are not among the most restrictive subcultures in the country.

(3) Insofar as a study of age cohorts can simulate changing trends, it is certainly the case that most Americans and ethnic groups have become more "liberal" in their sexual norms through the years. But with the exception of the Irish Catholics, the rate of change among Catholics does not seem to have been any more rapid than the rate of change among other groups in the society.

But still, there have been changes—striking ones—in American sexual attitudes in recent decades. It is less clear that there have been notable changes in sexual behavior. If indeed there was a sexual revolution at all, it may well have occurred in the late 1700s. The principal behavioral changes in the last two decades may be merely the result of the fact that effective and readily available birth control systems have enabled young people to go a little bit further in their explorations of intimacy now than they would have in the 1930s and 1940s. Chastity and self-restraint have never been particularly popular virtues. What has changed—and it is not unimportant—is attitudes, public and private, to sexual behavior. That which used to be strongly condemned now can be tolerated and justified more easily than in the past—though it does not necessarily follow that the behavior will become any more frequent. Neither fornication nor adultery were invented in the present era, and though it may have taken the present era to advance the best arguments for it, such behavior was not really considered "wrong." It may also be the case that as in other major shifts in public and private attitudes toward sex, the one we are witnessing today may be merely a swing of the pendulum. A return to more resrictive norms may recur at some time in the future.

Whatever the final judgment one would make in the "revolution" of sexual attitudes, the question still remains whether this revolution has by itself a notable impact on Catholic religious behavior. If the perspective mentioned in the previous paragraph—that revolution in attitudes was not a revolution in behavior—is correct, then one could hazard the guess that only those sexual norms which involve most people frequently are going to have a notable effect on religious behavior. Since most Catholics are heterosexual, changing attitudes on homosexuality, one would hypothesize, would not have much effect on Catholic devotion or institutional loyalty. Similarly, since most Catholics, like most other Americans, are faithful to their spouses (at least most of the time), it is unlikely that the apparent increase in tolerance for extramarital sex would notably influence Catholic church attendance. On the other hand, one could easily speculate that those aspects of "permissiveness" which would impinge on fertility might have a very considerable effect on Catholic religious behavior.

In *Catholic Schools in a Declining Church* the present author and his colleagues argued that virtually all the decline in Catholic religious devotion and practice in the years after the Second Vatican Council could be accounted for by the influx of a younger age group and by the changing attitudes among the rest of the Catholic population on birth control and papal authority. This conclusion was vigorously challenged by a number of bishops, editorial writers, columnists, and Catholic commentators, and by some sociologists—though by no socioligists trained in the techniques of longitudinal analysis that were used in the report.

"Secularization" and "the sexual revolution" were cited by virtually all the hostile critics as the "real" reasons for Catholic religious decline. Rarely was there any specification of what "secularization" meant, so it was impossible to test the impact of such a vague and undefined concept. However, in the reanalysis of the NORC data it was possible to determine whether there was a Catholic "sexual revolution" between 1963 and 1974, and whether that sexual revolution did account for the decline of Catholic religious practice instead of the highly specific issues of birth control and papal authority.

First of all, there was indeed a dramatic change in Catholic sexual attitudes in the years between the two NORC studies (Table 3). In 1963, 69 percent of the Catholics in the country thought that the ideal family size involved more than 3 children. This proportion fell in the ensuing decade a full 30 percentage points. In 1963, a little better than one-quarter (29 percent) of the respondents thought that husband and wife might have sexual intercourse for pleasure alone. More than half agreed to that proposition strongly in 1974. Finally, 23 percent in 1963 rejected strongly the notion that a family should have as many children as possible and God will provide for them, while the

TABLE 3

THE CATHOLIC "SEXUAL REVOLUTION" 1963-1974

	1963	1974
Ideal family size more than 3 children	69%	39%
Husband and wife may have sexual intercourse for pleasure alone (agree strongly)	29%	51%
A family should have as many children as possible and God will provide for them (disagree strongly)	23%	58%

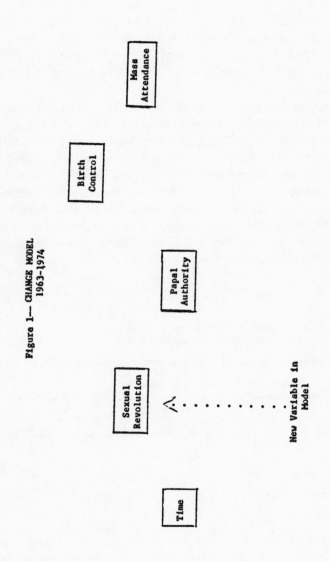

Figure 1— CHANGE MODEL
1963-1974

Mass
Attendance

Birth
Control

Papal
Authority

Sexual
Revolution

Time

New Variable in
Model

223

proportion a decade later had risen to 58 percent. There has been, therefore, very substantial, indeed monumental, shift in Catholic attitudes on family size, on the purpose of sexual intercourse, and on responsible child-bearing in the interlude between the two NORC studies. There was indeed a sexual revolution and a very big one between 1963 and 1974 among American Catholics.

It therefore becomes necessary to revise the social change model and examine the possibility that the sexual revolution led to the changes in attitudes on papal authority and birth control which were responsible for the decline in religious devotion. Certainly on *a priori* grounds one would expect that there would be powerful relationships between such traditional components of "Catholic" sexual ethics as number of children, the purpose of intercourse, and trust in God on the one hand and religious devotion on the other. Thus the modification in the model portrayed in Figure 1 seems appropriate.

TABLE 4

IMPACT OF "SEXUAL REVOLUTION"
ON CATHOLIC RELIGIOUS ATTENDANCE

(Mass Attendance decline 21% points between 1963 and 1974)

Proportion of Change Accounted For

	Old Model	New Model
Cohort	.20	.20
Birth control attitude	.46	.40
Papal authority attitude	.34	.25
Sexual revolution	*	.15
Total change accounted for	1.00	1.00

*not in model

However, in fact, the explanatory power of the sexual revolution in accounting for the decline in mass attendance is not very great. It accounts for only 15 percent of the decline, taking 6 percentage points away from birth control attitude and 9 percentage points away from papal authority (Table 4). If one leaves out the impact of cohort, one can say that even in the new model the *Humanae Vitae* variables—birth control and papal authority—account for 65 percent of the change, the sexual revolution only for 15 percent of the change in church attendance.

To confirm the relative importance of birth control and papal authority as opposed to sexual revolution, one can display, as in Table 5, the correlations between these variables and both mass and communion reception in 1974. There is no significance at all between belief in sex for pleasure and either mass or communion and only small correlations between ideal family size and communion and having as many children as possible and mass. Only the relationship between communion and as many children as possible achieves .2; but all four of the relationships between birth control and papal authority, on the one hand, and mass attendance and communion reception, on the other, are in excess of .24.

In panel C of Table 5, incidentally, there is yet more confirmation for the argument that the sexual revolution *per se* cannot be blamed for the declining religious practice. There are no statistically significant correlations between attitudes on divorce, extramarital sex, homosexuality, birth control information for teens, and attendance at an X-rated movie on the one hand and church attendance on the other. Only on the matter of premarital sex (which is quite closely connected with attitudes on birth control, as was demonstrated in *Catholic Schools in a Declining Church*) is there a statistically significant negative coefficient between church attendance and sexual permissiveness. Catholics, in other words, are changing their attitudes on sexuality, but these changes, with one or two exceptions, are having relatively little influençe on changing patterns of religious devotion, be-

TABLE 5

A. CORRELATIONS BETWEEN "SEXUAL REVOLUTION"
ITEMS AND 1974 RELIGIOUS BEHAVIOR

	Mass	Communion
Ideal family size	*	.17
As many children as possible	.16	.20
Sex for pleasure	*	*

*Correlations not statistically significant

B. CORRELATIONS BETWEEN "HUMANAE VITAE" ITEMS
AND RELIGIOUS BEHAVIOR

	Mass	Communion
Birth control attitude	.26	.28
Papal authority attitude	.24	.24

C. STANDARDIZED CORRELATIONS BETWEEN CHURCH ATTENDANCE FOR CATHOLICS
AND SEXUAL ATTITUDES IN NORC GENERAL SOCIAL SURVEY

Sexual Attitudes	Church Attendance
Age	*
Easier divorce laws	*
Approve extramarital sex	*
Approve premarital sex	.27
Approve homosexuality	*
Approve birth control information for teens	*
Seen an x-rated movie	*

*Correlations not statistically significant.

226

cause the attitudes themselves do not correlate (any more, at any rate) with religious devotion. To put the matter somewhat differently and perhaps more strikingly, there is no discernible difference between devout and nondevout Catholics in their notions of ideal family size, whether you may have sex for pleasure, whether homosexuality is good or evil, whether birth control information should be dispensed to teenagers, and whether there ought to be easier divorce laws. *The birth control issue alone seems to be the occasion for the substantial decline in religious behavior which has occurred among American Catholics since the early 1960s.*

Thus the first of our questions on the sexuality issue has been answered. The "revolution" in sexual permissiveness (to use what I think is the most precise label for it) has affected Catholics, as it has affected all other Americans; but it has not affected their church practice with the single exception of the changing attitudes on birth control.

The second question is somewhat more difficult to answer because we do not have data available to show how the unchurched feel about the Catholic Church's sexual stand, though we know from data cited in previous chapters that there is a negative correlation between traditional sexuality and all the forms of church relationship that we have studied. Humankind, in the Western world, at any rate, has gone through an enormous change in its thinking about sex since the end of the Second World War. This change can be explained in part, perhaps, by the psychoanalytic revolution; but a more important explanation would seem to be that Western humankind has finally discovered that it is truly in a totally new situation sexually. The human race may be sustained in its present size with relatively little childbearing activity; the family function as an economic unit passing on family property and as an economic exchange system sorting out relationships in a rural society has come to an end. Sex and procreation have never been completely identified in the human condition, and they can never be completely separated; yet long life expectancy, low infant mortality rates, and certain and reasonably safe means of birth control have forced humankind into a condition for which its ethical systems were not prepared. The ethical systems are not necessarily deficient. After all, this new condition is less than a hundred years old even in the most advanced countries of the world.

The net result of the demographic revolution (and this, as I have said before, is probably the only real revolution of all those about which we hear on television) is to leave humankind, or at least the Western variety, confused. The articulation of the traditional moral wisdom simply no longer seems pertinent or even tolerable given the extraordinary change in the condition in which humans find themselves. On the other hand, no new wisdom has appeared on the scene to provide humans with the meaning they need to interpret their sexual behavior and guidelines by which they might live their sexual lives in some kind of relative peace and happiness. Those ethical visions which purport to be new (such as "The Playboy Philosophy" in its more sophisticated variants) are in fact not new at all, but are revived versions of ancient pagan hedonism. They may be of some use in justifying quick tension release, but they are certainly not useful as roadmaps through the tangled thicket of human emotions.

One might be tempted to say that whoever wins the race to put together a viable new sexual ethic which will take into account the perduring wisdom of the ancient tradition and the almost totally original circumstances in which modern Western humans find themselves will receive an enormous prize of human loyalty and gratitude. I do not make this observation lightly; just now there don't seem to be any contestants entered into the competition, and humankind drifts through what may be its greatest sexual crisis without any guidance other than the old rigidities and the old hedonism.

If the Catholic Church could win the race—in which no one has yet entered—to articulate a new sexual wisdom, then one could readily imagine that its evangelization efforts could be quite successful. Since one can hardly anticipate a rearticulation of the Catholic sexual ethic in the near future, one must ask the

228

more modest question, can an evangelizing religion, doggedly preaching sexual norms which the majority of its own members reject, expect to succeed with others who are not its members, who are more "liberal" on sex than its members?

The appropriate answer seems to be that the evangelization efforts of such a denomination are not likely to be very successful. Quite simply, as long as the Catholic Church's official stand continues to be against birth control, it cannot reasonably expect its evangelization activities to be effective.

Finally, the third of our questions about the sexuality issue: Are there any hints in the data about the constructive direction in which the Church might go in attempts to rearticulate its sexual wisdom?

I began this phase of the analysis by assuming that successful human intimacy is necessarily a blend of affection and conflict. Far from destroying human intimacy, conflict makes it possible by enabling people to bring to the surface and deal effectively with the problems of their common life. As Louis Coser pointed out in his very wise *Social Conflict,* a relationship which has no conflict is one either of oppression or indifference. Furthermore, a relationship in which conflict is not structured within the broader goals of the relationship will be one that is deteriorating toward extinction. Somewhere in between—conflict subservient to the higher goals of the relationship—is the ideal in human intimacy.

We have one data set available (the 1977 alcohol study by NORC) which provides information on conflict and affection between husband and wife—information reported by the adolescent children of the marriage (along with other information about the marriage reported by both adolescents and parents). We hypothesized that that religious world view which might most appropriately be described as "Christian" was most effectively transmitted by parents to children in those circumstances in which both affection and conflict are obvious to the young people. In other words, if children perceive their parents' interactions as both affectionate and sometimes angry, the parents' Christian

229

world view will be more effectively transmitted to the children than under other circumstances.

The reasoning behind these hypothetical assumptions is admittedly intricate and complex. The data analyst rarely expects to find evidence which will support such an elaborate chain of ideas. Nevertheless, the implications for religion, sexuality, and for human relationship of the possibilities outlined in this train of thought are so important that it seemed very much worth the effort to find whether there was any support for our hypotheses.

McCready and I have developed a method for looking at the "ultimate value" or the "basic beliefs" of Americans, which is based on Clifford Geertz's definition of religion:*

"A religion is: a system of symbols which acts to establish powerful, pervasive, and long-lasting moods and motivations in men by formulating conceptions of a general order of existence and clothing these conceptions with such an aura of factuality that the moods and motivations seem uniquely realistic.[1]

"A religion, according to this definition, serves both as a 'model for' and a 'model of' reality. A 'model of' reality presents relationships in such a way as to render them apprehensible. It expresses the structure of the relationships in synoptic form. A 'model for' reality is the reverse of the above: it creates relationships according to some previously attained apprehension of reality. An architectural structure and a set of blueprints can serve as an analogy for these two concepts. We might go through the structure and chart all the physical relationships we could find and produce a set of blueprints which would be a 'model of' the structure. On the other hand, we might know what kind of building was needed and sit down to draw out all the physical

---

* The 16 paragraphs following the definition are taken from William C. McCready with Andrew M. Greeley, *The Ultimate Values of the American Population.* Beverly Hills, Cal.: Sage Publications, 1976.

relationships on paper, in which case the blueprints become a guide or a 'model for' the final structure.

"A religion, and especially the symbols associated with it, is 'ultimate' in the sense that it provides both an interpretation, or a 'model of,' for dealing with the most complex human problems such as suffering, death, and the experience of limitation at many levels, as well as a conviction that reality is interpretable, or a 'model for.' This dual function gives religious symbols varying degrees of power in different societies and makes them complex objects of investigation.

"Man is very vulnerable in this world. Many things can harm him and he is well aware of the fact that physical existence ends at some time in the future. Social injustices and evils of all kind abound, and the evidence would seem to indicate that there is nothing much in the way of a plan for humankind. However, man is able to do more than react to a 'model of' which is presented before him; he is able to create a 'model for' from that which he observes. Religion, as Geertz notes, is the modest assumption that God is not mad; or, to put it more prosaically, it is the modest—but very critical—assumption that existence is not pure chaos. Even to say that life is ultimately absurd is at least to develop a proposition that itself has meaning and according to which one can shape one's reactions to the most basic questions of life. If the universe is ultimately uninterpretable— even with the interpretation of despair—then the underpinnings of all other attempts at interpretation are removed and one is caught in cosmic chaos, a situation which is intolerable for virtually all human adults.

"We can leave aside for the purposes of the present work whether there are humans who are able to live and work without essaying some tentative answers to the questions of good and evil, life and death, comedy and tragedy. It is surely the case that most people cannot, and it may well be the case, as Edward Shils, following Durkheim, has suggested, that no "serious" person can avoid asking ultimate questions.[2] But our purpose in this present work is not to ask whether every human has a religion in the Geertzian sense, but rather to determine what the religious interpretive scheme is of that overwhelming majority of Americans who do at least on occasion ask questions of ultimate meaning.

"Like all notions that are of critical importance, humankind tends to express its religions in symbols, and not only or merely in prose propositions. Images, pictures, stories, and rituals are incarnated religious insights which purport to explain what ultimate life, reality, and the world are all about. In the present work, we have not been able to trace in any great detail the linkage between symbol and interpretation—though God is clearly the central, the 'privileged' symbol (to use Paul Ricoeur's word) of most religious systems.[3] Tell me who your God is and I will know what you believe about life and death, cosmos and chaos, good and evil. Our limited purpose at the present time, however, is to sketch an overview of the prose statements of the basic beliefs (or ultimate values) of the American population. At a later date it may be possible to go more deeply into the question of the relationship between religious symbols and the insights they express and incarnate—though that would be stretching the wisdom and the techniques of survey research far beyond their present capacities.

"The second tradition which has influenced our work is the study of the transmission of values and, in particular, the very limited work that has been done on the transmission of religious values. Caplowitz noted in the early 1960s that those who had left their childhood religion frequently came from families where there was a high level of tension either between the parents or between parent and child.[4] Kotre was able to explain much of the variance in religious self-definition of graduate students in terms of their childhood experiences in the family interaction network.[5] Greeley (*The Denominational Society*) notes similar phenomena.[6] Finally, McCready, in his research on religious socialization among American Catholics, was able to explain approximately 60 percent of the variance in mass attendance, and lesser amounts in other behaviors and attitudes, with a socialization model.[7] Particularly important in the model was the religious behavior of the father, and, in the case of the male respondents, the quality of the relationship between mothers and fathers. Since he was dealing with three generations, McCready was able to replicate the findings of his first- and second-generation relationships with the relationships between the second and third generations. (In a later work, McCready and his wife suggested that basic world view was strongly related to sexual identity and that one's view of the nature of the cosmos and one's view of oneself as a male or female may well be acquired at the same time, if not by the same process.)[8]

"We do not yet have the resources to test this hypothesis, but in the present work we are able to ask (of our adult respondents) how the basic belief systems were influenced by their parents' behavior and how adults, in turn, transmit their basic beliefs to their adolescent children.

"It should be emphasized that our efforts are exploratory. We are engaged in what we believe is a radically new approach to the study of religion. Most of our measures and techniques are being used for the first time. Our analytic techniques are new in religious research. Our theoretical assumptions are still rough and unrefined—as are all assumptions before they are tried in the crucible of data collection. As in all preliminary exercises, wise researchers hope to profit from mistakes and are flattered if other researchers are able to go beyond what they have done. . . .

"Having decided to attempt to measure basic meaning systems, we were faced with the problem of what the likely sets of interpretation might be in American society. Since no one had approached this question before, there was no literature to fall back on for guidance. What was the possible range of responses to ultimate issues available to humankind in contemporary America—or, indeed, to humankind at any time in its history?

"We finally decided to take our cue from Paul Ricoeur's classic mixture of anthropology, archaeology, comparative religion, and philosophy, *The Symbolism of Evil*. According to Ricoeur, there have been four fundamental responses to ultimate questions of good and evil—the optimistic (which Ricoeur sees in Egyptian religion), the pessimistic (as represented by Mesopotamian religious symbols), the fatalistic (to be found in post-Homeric Greece), and the hopeful (as manifest by the Israelites' religion).

"The optimistic world view sees reality as ultimately good, though tinged with some sadness and evil which are not of major moment. The pessimistic sees the world as a cruel, hostile, and unsympathetic place. The fatalistic perspective shares the same grim view, but, unlike the pessimistic, sees little point in attempting to deal with or manipulate the hostile powers which dominate the cosmos. Finally, the hopeful perspective does not deny the cosmic battle between good and evil, nor the apparent success of evil in the battle, but believes in the precarious triumph of good; in this perspective, death, evil, and suffering have much to say, but they do not completely possess the last word.

"It is obviously a long way from Ricoeur's typology to a survey questionnaire, but we theorized that there might be six major ultimate value responses among modern Americans. The optimistic thrust, we speculated, might be divided into an uncomplicated religious optimism and an equally uncomplicated nonreligious or secular optimism. (We do not use "uncomplicated" in a pejorative sense, but rather to indicate that the belief system tends to minimize the problem of evil.) The pessimistic approach might be either fatalistic and resigned (like the Stoics) or angry. Between optimism and pessimism we hypothesized a neutral stance in which the person expressed gratitude for past benefits. The hopeful approach, much as in the past, would tip the scales ever so slightly to favor good in the cosmic war in heaven. Thus, the six possible interpretive responses to life problems would look something like this:

(1) Religious optimism: 'God will take care of everything, so there is no need to worry.'

(2) Secular optimism: 'Everything will turn out for the best somehow.'

(3) Grateful acceptance: 'We must be thankful for the good

things that have happened to us despite the bad that we
have to endure.'

(4) Anger: 'It is unfair and unjust that we should have to
suffer.'

(5) Resignation: 'There is nothing that can be done; what
will be will be.'

(6) Hopefulness: 'There is no denying the evil of what is
happening, but the last word has not been said yet.' "

In the NORC alcohol study, two of the basic belief "vignettes"
were used. In a change from the previous wordings of the questions, the respondents were asked to rate themselves on a five-
point scale with reference to each of the possible responses to
the vignettes (Table 6). There are, incidentally, remarkable
similarities in the responses of adults and adolescents on the
twelve items of the two vignettes, with anger and fatalism being
the lowest for both generations and hopefulness and gratitude
being the highest.

The correlations for the specified items in each of the scales
are remarkably high (save for the two angry items, whose correlation was a relatively low .18). Since the four optimism (two
secular and two religious) items correlated highly, they were
combined in one optimism scale. Thus there was available for
the alcohol research five different "world-view" scales: Optimistic, Grateful, Hopeful, Angry, and Resigned (Table 7). There
was also a high correlation among the three most explicitly religious scales, optimistic, hopeful, grateful. (Not unsurprising,
because all three are part of the traditional religious responses
to injustice, tragedy, and death.) More important for the general
theoretical concern on ultimate values and for the purposes of
this chapter, there were strong correlations between parents and
children in both the Optimism and Hope world views, a moderate
correlation between parents and children in the Angry world
views. Thus our vignettes not only tap a dimension of human
religious perspective, they also tap a dimension that is transmitted from parents to children.

I assumed that it would be among families where both affec-

TABLE 6

BASIC BELIEF VIGNETTES

(% very close to respondent's feelings)

	Adults	Adolescen
Here is a situation in which some people actually find themselves. Imagine that one of your parents is dying a slow and painful death. How close is each of the following statements to your own reaction to such a situation?		
A. They are in pain now, but they will be peaceful soon. (Secular Optimism)	35	29
B. Everything that happens is God's will and cannot be bad. (Religious Optimism)	18	21
C. There is nothing to do but wait for the end. (Resignation)	15	13
D. This waiting is inhuman for them; I hope it ends soon. (Angry)	39	27
E. We can at least be thankful for the good life we have have had together. (Grateful)	51	54
F. This is tragic, but death is not the ultimate end for us. (Hopeful)	42	32
Here is another situation in which some people actually find themselves, and we would like you to imagine that that it has happened to you. You have just visited your doctor and he has told you that you have less than a year to live. He has told you that your disease is incurable. How close is each of the following statements to your own reaction?		
A. It will all work out for the best somehow.	23	16
B. No one should question the goodness of God's decision about death.	18	20
C. There is nothing to do but wait for the end.	11	9
D. I am angry and depressed at the unfairness of it all.	23	15
E. I am thankful for the life that I have had.	49	49
F. I cannot explain why this has happened to me, but I still believe in God's love.	47	43

TABLE 7

INTERGENERATIONAL CORRELATIONS OF WORLD VIEW ITEMS

	OPTIMISM		
	Secular Optimism 2	Religious Optimism 1	Religious Optimism 2
Secular optimism 1	.26	.43	.25
Secular optimism 2		.58	.58
Religious optimism 1			.67
Religious optimism 2			

GRATEFUL

.42

HOPEFUL

.58

Angry

.18

RESIGNED

.58

TABLE 8

INTERCORRELATIONS OF BASIC BELIEF SYSTEM

	Hopeful	Grateful	Angry	Resigned
Optimistic	.62	.41	-.13	.39
Hopeful		.43	-.13	.08
Grateful			.03	.19
Angry				.26
Resigned				

237

TABLE 9

INTERGENERATIONAL CORRELATIONS IN BASIC BELIEFS

Hopeful	.35
Optimist	.36
Angry	.17
Resigned	.10
Grateful	.09

tion and anger is most easily expressed that one would find (a) higher levels of hopefulness among young people and (b) a more effective transmission of hopefulness from parents to adolescents. I argued in this fashion on the admittedly speculative grounds that hope is a world view that can look squarely and honestly at evil and still retain its capability of asserting that goodness is stronger than evil. In the family where affection is mixed with conflict, where affection is stronger, it seemed to me that one would find examples of hopefulness acted out every day, providing the model for a hopeful life. There was, to my surprise and delight, confirmation in the data for both speculations (Table 10). Those adolescents from more "intimate" families are also "more hopeful" (fifteen standardized points) than those from less intimate families. The difference becomes even larger when one also takes into account a combination of affection and quarreling in a family. The young people who grew up in "emotional" family environments (those in which there is both hugging and kissing "often" and quarreling "sometimes") are 15 standardized points above the mean on the hopeful score. Thus, though the differences are small in both cases, they are in the direction hypothesized by my speculations. Those who grow up in families where affection is freely displayed, and especially those who grow up in families where both affection and anger are freely displayed, are more likely to be hopeful than are other adolescents.

238

TABLE 10

FAMILY ATMOSPHERE AND BASIC BELIEF OF ADOLESCENT

(z scores)

	More Intimate[a]	Less Intimate	More Emotional[b]	Less Emotional
Hopeful	.10	-.05	.15	-.03
Optimistic	.01	-.01	.00	.00
Angry	.00	.00	.00	.00
Grateful	.10	-.04	.10	-.02
Resigned	-.08	.04	.00	.00

[a]Parents described by adolescent as "hugging and kissing" often.

[b]Parents described by adolescent as "hugging and kissing" often and as quarreling often or sometimes.

Moreover, it is precisely in intimate and "emotional" families that the variance in adolescent hopefulness is more adequately explained. Indeed, twice as much of the variance can be explained for those families who combine affection with anger than can be explained in those families which are low in both affection and anger. Most interestingly, in the "more emotional" families, the beta between parent hopefulness and adolescent hopefulness is rather weak—a .09 compared to the .30 of less emotional families (Tables 11-12). Hopefulness in these families is not generated so much by imitation of parental hopefulness as it is by other dynamics at work within the boundaries of family life that have been structured by both hugging and kissing and by quarreling. The religiousness of one of the spouses and the family affection (as reported jointly by parents and adolescents) have a much higher effect on hopefulness than either of these two factors does in less emotional families.

It would appear that in these "more emotional" families hopefulness is generated not so much in imitation of parental hopefulness as it is in experiencing a situation in which there is family

239

TABLE 11

EXPLANATIONS OF VARIANCE IN ADOLESCENT HOPEFULNESS

	More Intimate	Less Intimate	More Emotional	Less Emotional
Total variance explained	24%	14%	29%	16%
Parental hopefulness (betas)	.27	.31	.09	.30
Parental church attendance	.13	*	*	.09
Parent's spouses'church attendance	.13	.13	.46	.06
Family affection	.14	*	.22	.08
Quality of parental relationship	.24	*	.30	.06

*Not significant.

TABLE 12

EXPLANATION OF VARIANCE IN ADOLESCENT OPTIMISM

	More Intimate	Less Intimate	More Emotional	Less Emotional
Total variance explained	22%	16%	17%	18%
Parental optimism (betas)	.36	.20	.22	.32
Parental church attendance	.16	*	*	.12
Parent's spouse church attendance	*	.17	.18	.07
Family affection	.16	.14	.20	.13
Quality of parental relationship	.08	.09	.10	.09

240

affection despite the apparent contradiction of hugging and kissing on the one hand and quarreling on the other. Both family affection, which is a measure put together on the basis of observations of parents and adolescents both, and the quality of the relationship (which is a parent judgment) have much stronger effects on hopefulness in the "emotional" family than they do with the less emotional ones, quite possibly because the ability to maintain a good relationship in the midst of the confusion and chaos in the intimacy marked by both conflict and love creates an emotional and religious environment in which the young person finds there are grounds for him or her to feel hopeful about what goes on in the world.

The theory behind this section of the chapter is highly speculative, and the data are thin. But the data do fit the expectations and they fit in a way which seems to make intuitive sense. Young people growing up in a family environment in which both love and anger can be expressed and in which love and affection are strong despite the anger, indeed stronger because of it, are more likely to approach life with a hopeful perspective—that is, the perspective which is well aware of evil but also well aware of goodness, goodness which is ever so slightly stronger than evil.

The Good News, of course, is the Good News of hopefulness. The gospel does not deny the cross; it simply asserts that the resurrection is stronger than the cross. Developing a vision of hopefulness in adolescence is, one would assume, the primary purpose of all religious instruction and education. It turns out that such hopefulness is most effectively developed in families in which both sides of the intimacy coin—affection and conflict—are dealt with successfully. The church which could in some way sustain and support, reinforce and facilitate men and women seeking to grow in intimacy would be a church which had found a remarkable "technique" for evangelizing.

To go beyond the data to a higher level of abstraction, the most critical issue for a church (or for any belief system) trying to cope with the current sexual confusion is to develop a theory of human intimacy. To develop such a theory one need not abandon the prohibitions of the past, but one must do far more than merely repeat them. A persuasive, illuminating theory of intimacy, reinforced and validated by the traditional Christian symbols, would obviously be a powerful asset in an evangelization campaign. It may also be a *sine qua non.*

The melancholy truth is that there are very few efforts being made by anyone toward developing such a theory of intimacy. Most professional theologians are uninterested. The Catholic Theological Society of America, for example, issued a report, *Human Sexuality,* which has nothing to say on the subject, choosing, rather, to limit itself to new answers to traditional moral theological questions. At the Vatican Council III meeting at Notre Dame in 1977 between theologians and social scientists, the theologians downplayed the importance of the intimacy issue, many arguing that it was an "irrelevant" issue in the "Third World."* The American Catholic bishops, in their response to the CTSA paper, were content with rejecting the new answers to the old questions and reasserting the old answers. To take intimacy off the old agenda of "mortal sin," "venial sin," and "marriage" and put in on a new agenda of how one grows in skills of affection and conflict requires a decisive break with the old perspective. Few in the Catholic Church today seem prepared to do this.**

To go far beyond the data, but not beyond the self-evident facts of the present situation: *until the Church begins to develop a new agenda for intimacy, evangelization will be nothing more than occupational rehabilitation for troubled bishops, priests, and religious.*

---

* If one is to believe such theologians, the inhabitants of the Third World are more concerned about revolution and liberation than they are about intimacy. I suspect that such a position tells us far more about the theologians than it does about the Third World.

** For two foolish and futile attempts to move this new agenda, see my books *Sexual Intimacy* (Chicago: Thomas More Press, 1973) and *Love and Play* (New York: Seabury, paperback, 1977). These have been generally dismissed out of hand with the argument that "a priest doesn't know anything about sex."

Chapter Ten

CONCLUSION

THREE sets of summary remarks are appropriate for this conclusion:

1. The nature of American religion.
2. Areas for further investigation about American religion.
3. Implications for evangelization.

American Religion

There is very little left of conventional theories of sociology of religion. In Table 1, we can observe that educational attainment —critical to the secularizàtion and social class theories—simply has no importance at all in explaining any of the forms of religious affiliation or disaffiliation with which this book has been concerned. Furthermore, social attitudes, so dearly beloved by liberals who demand the Church be "relevant," also play no role in any of the models we have developed (except for a positive correlation between religious devotion and favorable attitudes on racial integration—exactly the opposite of what the "relevance" theory would have us expect). Age, on the other hand, does affect alienation, unchurchedness, and dissatisfaction (and also "non-marriage" disidentification). The younger are more likely to be alienated, more likely to be unchurched, more likely to be dissatisfied. The age correlation is generally not large, not nearly as large, for example, as spouse's religious-

TABLE 1

RELIGIOUS DISSIDENCE IN AMERICA

	Alienated	Unchurched	Dissatisfied	Disidentifiers*	"Communal"
Age	yes	yes	yes	no	no
Family of origin	yes	yes	yes	no	no
Family of procreation	yes	yes	yes	yes	no
Sex attitudes	yes	yes	yes	no	no
Belief	yes	yes	yes	no	no
Social attitudes	no	no	no	no	no
Anticlerical	no	yes	yes	no	no
Semons	yes	NAP**	yes	no	no
Parish services (activities, counseling)	no	NAP	yes	no	no
Education	no	no	no	no	no

*Marriage disidentifiers—the majority group. Others are like the unchurched.

**NAP = not applicable.

244

ness; but it is consistent enough to require comment. Are young people less religious because they are young? In that case they may become more religious as they grow older. Or is it because they are members of a generation which has had special experiences inclining them to be religiously disaffiliated? In that case they may or may not change but at least are not harbingers of the future. Or, finally, are the young religiously unaffiliated or disaffiliated because they represent some long-term turnaway from religion?

The evidence in Chapter 7, while inconclusive, casts doubt on the "long-term trend" explanation. The young are no less likely to believe in life after death and are, in fact, even more likely to report mystical experience of the "twice born" variety. Sociologist Robert Wuthnow, in an ingenious article in the *American Sociological Review*,[1] concludes that the second explanation—a special generational experience—is the most probable. The generation that matured during the late 1960s and early 1970s had certain special experiences which inclined them to be less religious. (And, as I noted in an earlier chapter, the young are also more likely to be politically unaffiliated, as well as religiously unaffiliated.) Wuthnow, however, did not distinguish between Protestant and Catholic young people. My colleagues, William McCready and Christian Wells Jacobsen, and I speculated that there might be differences between Protestants and Catholics.

At Wuthnow's suggestion (in private correspondence) we decided to explore the possibilities of controlling his model for denomination, using two of the NORC General Social Surveys (1973 and 1975). A number of authors have argued (Johnson, Lewis, and Sena-Rivera, 1976) that in fact the Catholic birth control crisis is too simple an explanation, and that Catholics were merely showing the effects of "secularization" that had affected Protestants earlier. Catholics, in other words, were "catching up" in their secularization. To translate this argument into Wuthnow's model, one would hypothesize a higher "trend exposure" (T) impact on religious behavior for Catholics than for

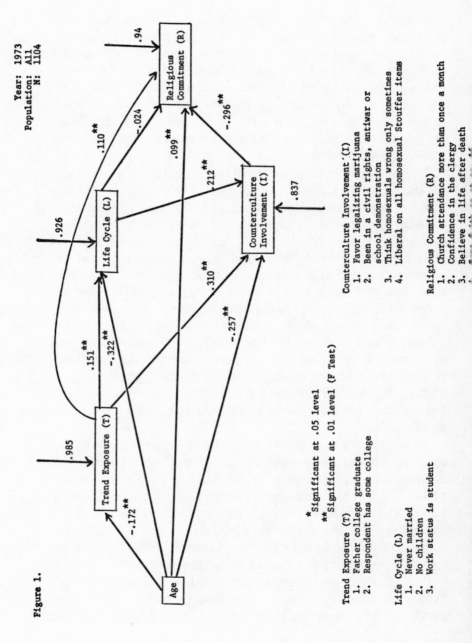

Figure 1.

Year: 1973
Population: All
N: 1104

*Significant at .05 level
**Significant at .01 level (F Test)

Trend Exposure (T)
1. Father college graduate
2. Respondent has some college

Life Cycle (L)
1. Never married
2. No children
3. Work status is student

Counterculture Involvement (I)
1. Favor legalizing marijuana
2. Been in a civil rights, antiwar or
   school demonstration
3. Think homosexuals wrong only sometimes
4. Liberal on all homosexual Stouffer items

Religious Commitment (R)
1. Church attendance more than once a month
2. Confidence in the clergy
3. Believe in life after death

246

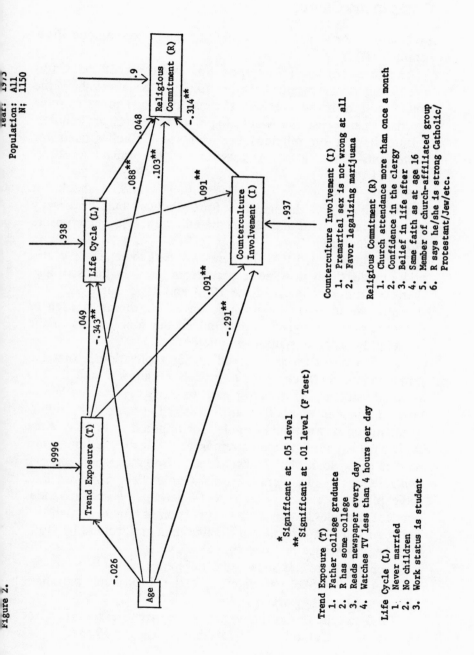

Trend Exposure (T)
1. Father college graduate
2. R has some college
3. Reads newspaper every day
4. Watches TV less than 4 hours per day

Life Cycle (L)
1. Never married
2. No children
3. Work status is student

Counterculture Involvement (I)
1. Premarital sex is not wrong at all
2. Favor legalizing marijuana

Religious Commitment (R)
1. Church attendance more than once a month
2. Confidence in the clergy
3. Belief in life after
4. Same faith as at age 16
5. Member of church-affiliated group
6. R says he/she is strong Catholic/
   Protestant/Jew/etc.

*Significant at .05 level
**Significant at .01 level (F Test)

Crisis in the Church

Protestants—or at least one as high as the impact among Protestants (T-R).

An alternative "cyclic" interpretation would suggest that Catholic young people would be more likely to be affected by the counterculture revolt precisely because they had more to rebel against. In this case one would hypothesize a stronger counterculture impact on religious behavior for Catholics than for Protestants—or at least one as strong as the impact for Protestants (I-R).

Finally, if what one is dealing with is "random shock," it would be likely that the age effect for Catholics would be directly on religious behavior and less mediated by either trend exposure or counterculture.

It should be noted that the items we used to replicate Wuthnow's model differ in some respects from the ones he used; also there are different items in the 1973 and 1975 surveys. (Incidentally, we did a factor analysis for all the items in each of our models and discovered that indeed the four factors in the model did cluster as Wuthnow hypothesized.)

The first result to be observed in our replication is that the parameters of both our general models (Figures 1 and 2) are strikingly similar, for the most part, to those reported by Wuthnow, and in some cases they are virtually the same. With different items on two national samples (as opposed to his Bay Area sample), his paradigm seems remarkably durable, although our models show somewhat higher direct correlations between age and religious commitment than his. Our models, however, lack the explanatory power of his model—perhaps because his independent variables have a higher proportion of "fundamentalistic" items, such as the "creation of the first man and woman by God" and the importance of "following God's will."

Secondly, there are substantial differences in both years between the Catholic paradigm and the Protestant paradigm (Figures 3-6). They are as follows:

(1) The relationship between age and trend exposure is not significant for Catholics in 1975 (though it is for 1973).

248

Figure 3

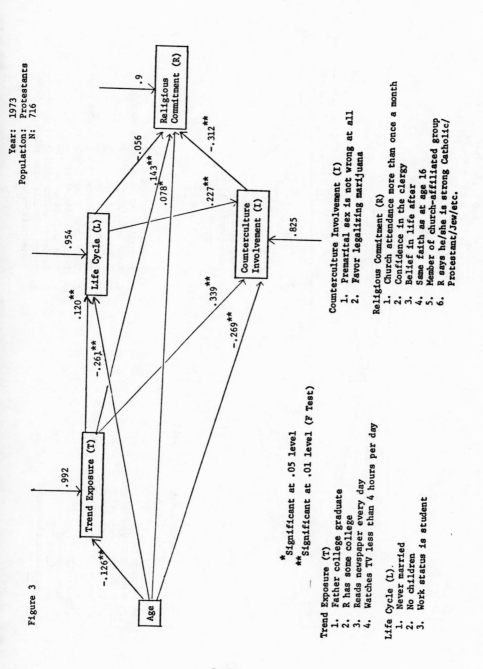

Trend Exposure (T)
1. Father college graduate
2. R has some college
3. Reads newspaper every day
4. Watches TV less than 4 hours per day

Life Cycle (L).
1. Never married
2. No children
3. Work status is student

*Significant at .05 level
**Significant at .01 level (F Test)

Counterculture Involvement (I)
1. Premarital sex is not wrong at all
2. Favor legalizing marijuana

Religious Commitment (R)
1. Church attendance more than once a month
2. Confidence in the clergy
3. Belief in life after
4. Same faith as at age 16
5. Member of church-affiliated group
6. R says he/she is strong Catholic/
   Protestant/Jew/etc.

249

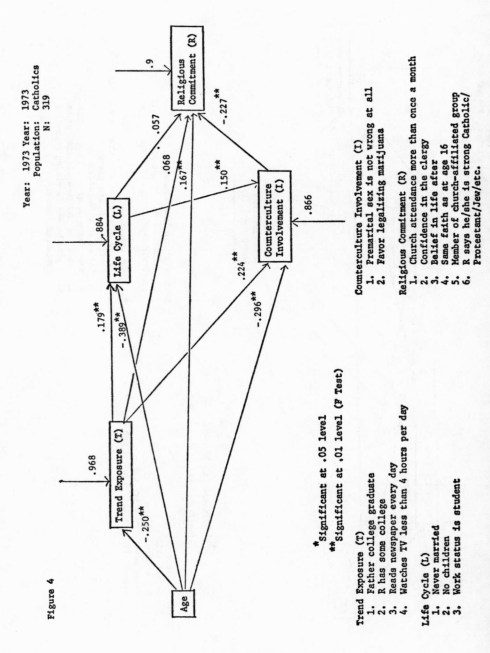

Figure 4

Year: 1973 Year: 1973
Population: Catholics
N: 319

*Significant at .05 level
**Significant at .01 level (F Test)

Trend Exposure (T)
1. Father college graduate
2. R has some college
3. Reads newspaper every day
4. Watches TV less than 4 hours per day

Life Cycle (L)
1. Never married
2. No children
3. Work status is student

Counterculture Involvement (I)
1. Premarital sex is not wrong at all
2. Favor legalizing marijuana

Religious Commitment (R)
1. Church attendance more than once a month
2. Confidence in the clergy
3. Belief in life after
4. Same faith as at age 16
5. Member of church-affiliated group
6. R says he/she is strong Catholic/
   Protestant/Jew/etc.

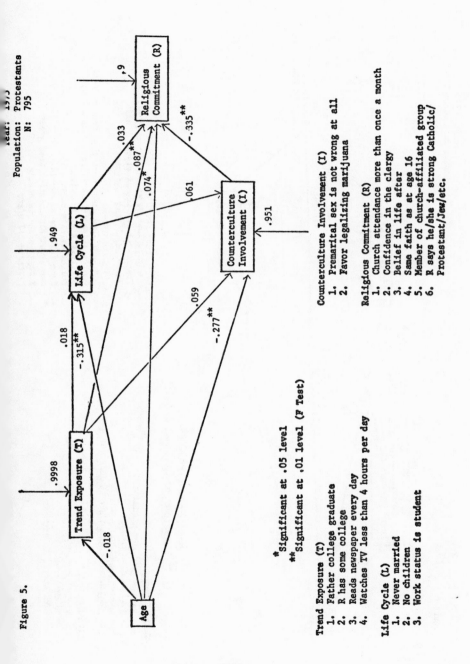

Figure 5.

Religious Commitment (R)

.9

Life Cycle (L)

.949

.033

.087**

.074*

.061

Counterculture Involvement (I)

.951

-.335**

Trend Exposure (T)

.9998

.018

-.315**

.059

-.277**

Age

-.018

*Significant at .05 level
**Significant at .01 level (F Test)

Trend Exposure (T)
1. Father college graduate
2. R has some college
3. Reads newspaper every day
4. Watches TV less than 4 hours per day

Life Cycle (L)
1. Never married
2. No children
3. Work status is student

Counterculture Involvement (I)
1. Premarital sex is not wrong at all
2. Favor legalizing marijuana

Religious Commitment (R)
1. Church attendance more than once a month
2. Confidence in the clergy
3. Belief in life after
4. Same faith as at age 16
5. Member of church-affiliated group
6. R says he/she is strong Catholic/
   Protestant/Jew/etc.

251

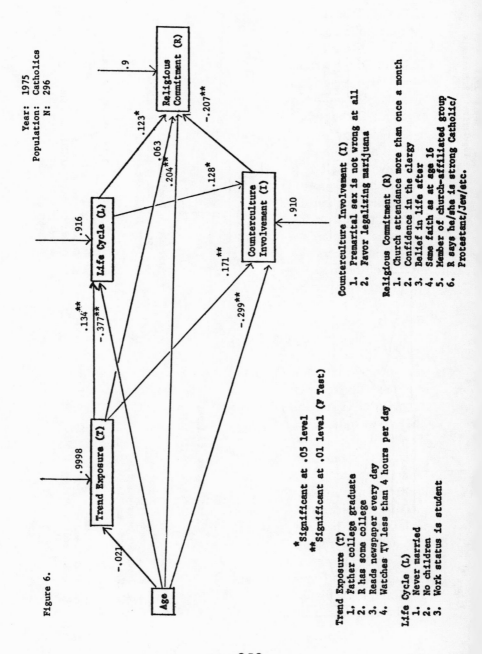

Figure 6.

Year: 1975
Population: Catholics
N: 296

*Significant at .05 level
**Significant at .01 level (F Test)

Trend Exposure (T)
1. Father college graduate
2. R has some college
3. Reads newspaper every day
4. Watches TV less than 4 hours per day

Life Cycle (L)
1. Never married
2. No children
3. Work status is student

Counterculture Involvement (I)
1. Premarital sex is not wrong at all
2. Favor legalizing marijuana

Religious Commitment (R)
1. Church attendance more than once a month
2. Confidence in the clergy
3. Belief in life after
4. Same faith as at age 16
5. Member of church-affiliated group
6. R says he/she is strong Catholic/
   Protestant/Jew/etc.

252

(2) The T-R relationship is significant for Protestants and not for Catholics.

(3) The I-R relationship is significant for both groups, but the relationship is stronger for Protestants than for Catholics.

(4) The direct relationship between age and religious behavior is significant for both Catholics and Protestants but much stronger for Catholics.

It should be noted that even though two different samples were used and different items went into the construction of the compositive variable in each sample, these last three observations are true of both samples.

Minimally one must conclude that there are very different dynamics at work in the Protestant model than are at work in the Catholic model. Thus in the 1973 Protestant model all paths are significant except the L-R path, while for Catholics only the lower half of the model provides significant paths into R (Age-R, I-R). The age impact, in other words, tends to be much more direct on R and not to be mediated by I, L, and T for Catholics.

There is, then, no evidence for either the "cyclical" or the "secular" explanations of Catholic religious decline during the 1960s. On the contrary, the models in Figures 4 and 6 are compatible with a "random shock" explanation.

It is possible to tentatively test further the "random shock" explanation of Catholic decline, using the 1975 NORC General Social Survey data. Questions were asked about both birth control and divorce (though they were not the same questions reported in *Catholic Schools in a Declining Church*). If one uses the marijuana item as a counterculture indicator and a scale composed of the birth control, divorce, and premarital sex items, one is able to construct a four-variable model (Figure 7) to test the relationship between age (A), counterculture (I), sexual change (S), and religious commitment (R). If one compares Figure 7 with Figures 5 and 6, it becomes apparent that the relationship between I and R is diminished but remains significant for Protestants in Figure 7. It is no longer significant for Catholics. The correlation between A and R for Catholics is cut in

Crisis in the Church

half when S intervenes between A and R. In effect, Wuthnow's model continues to work well for Protestants but seems to have little applicability for Catholics. Neither T, L, nor I have any direct impact on R for Catholics and there is a direct relationship between A and R among Catholics but not among Protestants. Furthermore, the indirect effects of A on R are all channeled through S. Trend exposure, counterculture, and life cycle, in other words, may play an important part in Protestant devotional behavior, but changing sexual attitudes seem to be the decisive factor for Catholic devotional behavior. The "random shock" theory seems to be sustained.

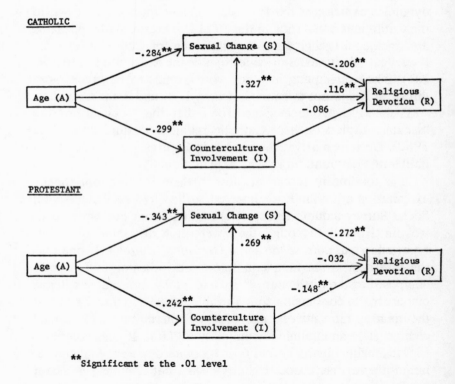

**Significant at the .01 level

Figure 7--Comparison between Catholic and Protestant Relationships between Age, Counterculture Involvement, Sexual Change, and Religious Devotion.

"Secularization," "social class," "relevance," then, simply are not even remotely adequate explanations of American religious affiliation and disaffiliation. The socialization model, foreshadowed by John Kotre and clearly enunciated by William Mc-Cready, is vastly more useful in approaching the phenomenon of American religion. Religious behavior is "learned" behavior. Americans "learn" to be religious or not from their parents and their spouses; and that "learning" is affected by such things as doctrinal beliefs, sexual attitudes, attitudes toward the clergy, and, for Roman Catholics at any rate, sermons. However, with the exception of "dissatisfaction" (on which attitudes toward clerical performance·are quite important), the "current attitudes" of Americans are considerably less important to explain their religious behavior than is the religiousness of their families, and particularly their spouses.

Note well that these last sentences are based on "net" comparisons. Even taking into account, for example, the fact that those·with spouses who are low on religiousness measures are also more likely to be low on belief in, let us say, life after death, the religiousness of the spouse is far more important than belief in life after death even when the effect of one on the other is taken into account.

It is the family of procreation, the family in which one participates as a husband or wife, that really matters. In most cases that family accounts for more of the variance in religious behavior than all the other variables put together. Perhaps the most effective proof of the importance of the family in American religiousness is the fact that the vast majority of the religious disidentifiers are those who entered religiously mixed marriage— apparently with someone more strongly committed to his-her denomination than the disidentifier was to his/her denomination. Marriage and religion seem linked inseparably.

The reader might be tempted to say that this observation is self-evident, that no one requires the dense text and elaborate multivariate models of the kind reproduced in this volume to establish it. I would respond that it has not been self-evident, apparently, either to sociologists of religion or to evangelization enthusiasts. Sociologists of religion have paid little attention to the "spouse religiousness" factor. Indeed, until McCready's breakthrough research, no serious attempt was made to look at the relationship between husband's religiousness and wife's. If you are busy dealing with such global concepts as secularization, of course, it hardly seems worth the effort to look at how religious a person's wife or husband may be.

Nor has there been, as far as I am aware, in any of the evangelization literature, an awareness that the proper target, indeed, the only meaningful target, for evangelization is the family unit. Virtually all the assumptions of evangelizationists are individualistic: you go out after the alienated or unchurched *person* with virtually no attention paid to the fact that most such persons are involved in an intimate relationship with a member of the opposite sex who has a decisive impact on the person's religious behavior. Catholic evangelization discussions have paid no attention to the potential disadvantages of evangelization on the family unit which might arise from the Church's teachings on marital intimacy.

If the importance of the spouse is simply a matter of common sense, then one would have to conclude that relatively little common sense has been displayed by sociologists of religion, religious leadership, and by writers and commentators who pontificate about religion in the secular and religious press. What counts religiously is not whether you have been "secularized" but rather to whom you are married.

What, then, is the most important religious influence in American life? The spouse. While we know little about the dynamics of religion and marriage, we do know that the impact of the spouse is virtually the same for men as for women, and that the happier the marriage the stronger the influence and the more likely the influence is to be in the direction of greater religiousness. When religious leaders, journalists, and theorists raise the question, "How do you make people more religious?" the best answer that can be offered on the basis of this volume is, "Make marriages happier."

Andrew Greeley

What Next for the Sociology of Religion?

Obviously, the first order of business for the sociology of religion (after books and articles of the secularization literature are tossed in the trash heap) is more research on the relationship between religion and family life with careful and precise measurements of the dynamics and the interactions by which parents influence their children religiously (and perhaps vice versa) and by which husbands and wives influence one another. There are three hints for such research in the materials presented in this book:

(1) The apparent mixed marriage phenomenon of choosing the affiliation of the religiously "stronger" spouse. Does this phenomenon have a parallel in other marriages? Does the spouse with the stronger convictions (either pro- or anti-religious) dominate in the religious family dialogue?

(2) What is the meaning of the hint that the happier the marriage the stronger and more positive is the couple's religious commitment? Are happier marriages more religious, are religious marriages happier, or is there some complex reciprocal causality?

(3) Finally, what is the relationship between religiousness and emotionality? We have observed that young people are more likely to have a "hopeful" worldview if both conflict and affection are openly displayed in the parental intimacy. Can one generalize from this phenomenon? McCready demonstrated several years ago that the quality of the husband-wife relationship affected the religiousness of the children, and that the critical aspect of that influence was the parental ability to combine successfully affection and conflict. Could one, without going much further beyond the existing data, speculate that the quality of parental sexual intimacy might be decisive in influencing the religiousness of their children—and perhaps even their own religiousness?

In fact, one may not even have to go through the complex reasoning used in our analysis of hopefulness to justify raising the question. If husband and wife influence each other religiously to the considerable extent demonstrated in this book, how can their sex life help but affect their religious behavior? The research issue is not whether there is a link between the bedroom and the church (for, after all, religion and sex have been closely linked through the course of human history) but rather how this relationship works. Again, if you are the prisoner of high-flown but vague secularization theory, this question will seem trivial.

The sociology of religion, if it abandons its secularization/social-class fixation, will also have to move beyond the rather inane dependent variables developed by Charles Glock, his students and colleagues. If the belief in life after death is a stable conviction, then one should know far more than we do about people's images of the nature of that life after death. If mystical experience is widespread in the society, then it ought to be studied in much greater detail. If there is relatively frequent contact with the dead, then that phenomenon should not be considered an "immoral" concern of those who study American religion. If more than half of the American public prays every day and there is a high positive correlation between prayer and psychological well-being, then much more detailed research on the prayer life of Americans is going to be essential. Finally, if conviction about the existence of God is unchanged among the American public, then it becomes pertinent to know far more about how Americans conceptualize the deity. (It is not enough to be given data from a question like whether God is a "person" or a "spirit" or a "force.")

Life after death, God, prayer, religious experience, religion as basic world view (in the Geertz sense of the word)—these are almost self-evidently important issues for the sociology of religion. One need only thumb through the index of the *Journal for the Scientific Study of Religion* or read the position papers issued by the staffs of the denominations (those which have them—Roman Catholicism doesn't need research staffs), peruse the editorials in such liberal journals as *America, The Commonweal, Christian Century,* or *Christianity in Crisis,* or look at the grants made by the religious funding agencies to realize that their importance is no more self-evident than is the importance of the religiousness of one's spouse.

Andrew Greeley

I am personally convinced that prayer, a hopeful worldview, and ecstatic experience are more important both intellectually and substantively than church affiliation and church attendance. Yet the dependent variables in this book are almost always church affiliation and church attendance. We do not have the intellectual tools or the data to cope with these other issues. They are not sufficiently important in the perspectives of denominational administrators, theologians, and journalists as to be considered pertinent topics for a book which focuses on evangelization. The purpose of evangelization, after all, is to get someone into your denomination and going to church regularly. There may be some lip service paid to personal conviction, to prayer, or to religious experience; but these are not goals that really count. After all, who would wish to organize a campaign to proclaim the Good News whose measure of success would be an increase in the levels of a hopeful worldview in American society?

The original Good News, of course, was about hope; but that hardly seems to be to the point.

Evangelization

The best that could be said at the end of this book about an enthusiastic evangelization campaign is that by itself it would represent a misplaced emphasis for three reasons.

(1) There is little evidence in our data of massive numbers of alienated or unchurched or dissatisfied or disidentified Americans who are eagerly awaiting recruitment by one or another denomination. There are, of course, potential candidates for religious recruitment, and they should not be ignored. However, the assumption that seems to lurk in much evangelization promotion of large numbers of recruits to be gained by intensive, enthusiastic campaigning simply does not fit the available evidence.

(2) American religious affiliation and disaffiliation is a complex, involved phenomenon. It is affected by experience in the

family in which you grew up, the family to which you presently belong, and by a variety of ethical, doctrinal, and ecclesiastical attitudes. One may have some success with a simple but intense evangelization campaign (an "evangelization year," for example), but the reasons why Americans are religious or irreligious do not admit, generally, of simple, easy, or direct treatment. Evangelization, if it is to be at all successful, must be a complex, long-term, sophisticated activity, one that is undertaken with full awareness that there will be far more failures than successes.

(3) If anything is evident at the conclusion of this book, it is that evangelization will only be more than slightly successful if it takes as its proper target the family unit. Very little is known about the religious dynamics of family life and the influence of the marital relationship on religion. If an individualistic evangelization would at best be carried on in a twilight of knowledge and understanding, then a family-oriented evangelization in the present state of our knowledge would be carried on in almost total darkness.

A Catholic evangelization campaign which fails to take into account the very serious problem of the Church's almost non-existent credibility in the area of sexual ethic will be, to put the matter mildly, a distinctly misplaced emphasis—especially given the importance of the family unit as the object of evangelization. An evangelization campaign which in effect says, "Join us and practice rhythm" will surely be a failure.

It is not my intention to ridicule the zeal of "evangelists," much less to question their preaching the gospel. This is an essential part of Christian activity. I strongly support both zeal and preaching (more zeal and better preaching), but I would submit that zeal ought to be well-informed and preaching intelligent. Much of the discussion in Roman Catholicism and in other denominations about evangelization does not seem either well-informed or intelligent, if only because the temptation seems to be to consider evangelization a single activity pursued enthusiastically without any regard for other complex and intricate aspects of American religious, social, and ethical life.

Even for the sophisticated members and staff of the Catholic hierarchy's Ad Hoc Committee on Evangelization the temptation to view evangelization as an activity that can be cut off both intellectually and organizationally from the other problems and difficulties of American Catholicism has been serious. At this writing, it is not clear to me how the Ad Hoc Committee will finally resolve its problem of role definition, how it will answer the critical question of the context that must be considered in planning an evangelization program.

As far as I'm concerned, the touchstone is sexuality. As is undoubtedly clear by now, I am convinced that any religious effort which does not seriously address the problems and the opportunities for religion in the current ambiguities of human sexuality is going to be a wasted effort. Yet the Ad Hoc Committee, indeed the whole American Catholic Church, would much prefer an evangelization from which sex could be excluded.

Enthusiasm, even naive, uninformed, unintelligent enthusiasm, has its merits; it will surely accomplish some limited goals, but it will not hold an organization together, it will not sustain an institution over the long haul, it will not bring Good News to the ends of the earth. It is no substitute for activity informed and directed by human intelligence. I do not wish to be thought of as condemning enthusiasm and the limited goals it can accomplish; I would simply say that both are inadequate and ultimately unworthy of any religious heritage that asserts it is appealing to the total human person. I think my stand is consistent with the Catholic Christian tradition, which has always viewed with great suspicion unintelligent and unenlightened enthusiasm.

Still, if you have nothing else to do and feel you must do something, a simplistic and enthusiastic evangelistic campaign probably does no one any great deal of harm and is as useful a technique for psychotherapy as many of the others that are available.

NOTES

CHAPTER ONE

1. Dean M. Kelley, *Why Conservative Churches Are Growing*, New York: Harper-Row, 1972.
2. Andrew M. Greeley, William C. McCready, Kathleen McCourt, *Catholic Schools in a Declining Church*, Kansas City, Missouri: Sheed & Ward, 1976.
3. Ronald A. Knox, *Enthusiasm*, New York: Oxford University Press, 1961.
4. Andrew M. Greeley, *Unsecular Man, the Persistence of Religion*, New York: Schocken Books, 1972. See also "Sociology and Theology: Some Methodological Questions," a paper delivered at the meetings of the Catholic Theological Society of America, Notre Dame, Indiana, May 27-June 1, 1977.
5. William C. McCready, "Faith of Our Fathers: A Study of the Process of Religious Socialization," Ph.D. dissertation, University of Illinois at Chicago Circle, 1972.
6. See Clifford Geertz, *Islam Observed*, New Haven: Yale University Press, 1968; and *The Interpretation of Cultures*, New York: Basic Books, 1973.
7. For an interesting discussion of the question of which stimuli we choose to focus on and the effect on us of our choices from the past, see John Kotre's *A View from the Border: A Social Psychological Study of Current Catholicism*, Chicago: Aldine, 1971.

CHAPTER TWO

1. Andrew M. Greeley, William C. McCready, Kathleen McCourt, *Catholic Schools in a Declining Church*, Mission, Kansas: Sheed and Ward, 1976.

2. Robert Wuthnow, "Recent Patterns of Secularization: A Problem of Generations?" *American Sociological Review,* 41 (1976):850-867.

3. Andrew M. Greeley, Christian Jacobsen, William C. McCready, "Pattern of Secularization: An Alternative Explanation for Catholics: A Comment on Wuthnow," submitted to the *American Sociological Review,* 1977.

4. John Kotre, *A View from the Border,* Chicago: Aldine, 1971.

5. William C. McCready, *Faith of Our Fathers,* Unpublished Ph.D. dissertation, University of Illinois at Chicago, 1972.

6. Andrew M. Greeley and Richard Schoenherr, *American Priests,* Chicago: NORC, 1971.

7. William C. McCready with Andrew M. Greeley, *The Ultimate Values of the American Population,* Beverly Hills, Cal.: Sage Publications, 1976.

CHAPTER FIVE

1. See Andrew M. Greeley, *The Communal Catholic,* New York: Seabury, 1976; and "Catholic Schools and the Two Churches," an address to the 74th annual Convention and Religion Education Congress of the National Catholic Educational Association, San Francisco, April 11-14, 1977.

CHAPTER SIX

1. See Charles Y. Glock and Rodney Stark, *Religion and Society in Tension.* Chicago: Rand McNally & Co., 1965.

2. Robert Withnow, "Recent Pattern of Secularization: A Problem of Generations?" *American Sociological Review* 41 (October 1976: 850-867.

3. See John Kotre, *View From the Border: A Social Psychological Study of Current Catholicism.* Chicago: Aldine Publishing Company, 1971; Joseph Zelan, "Religious Apostasy, Higher Education, and Occupational Choice," *Sociology of Education* 41 (Fall 1968):370-379; David Caplovitz, *The Religious Dropout: Apostasy among College Graduates,* Beverly Hills, Cal.: Sage Publications, 1977.

4. See Norman H. Nie, John Petrocik and Sidney Verba, *The Changing American Voter,* Cambridge, Mass: Harvard University Press, 1976; Joan Fee, "Political Continuity and Change," Chapter 4 in Andrew M. Greeley, William C. McCready, and Kathleen McCourt, *Catholic Schools in a Declining Church,* Kansas City: Sheed & Ward, 1976.

Crisis in the Church

CHAPTER EIGHT

1. C. Lincoln Johnson, J. David Lewis, and Jaime Sena-Rivera, "A Review of *Catholic Schools in a Declining Church* by Andrew M. Greeley, William McCready, and Kathleen McCourt" in *Contemporary Sociology: A Journal of Reviews*, 5 (November 1976): 806–808, p. 807.
2. *Ibid.*, p. 808.
3. The *Catholic Digest* surveys were reported in John L. Thomas, S.J., *Religion and the American People*, Westminster, Md.: Newman Press, 1963.
4. Walter Blumberg and Paul Schilder, "The Attitudes of Psychoneurotics Towards Death," *Psychoanalytic Review*, 23(1936).
5. G. K. Chesterton, "The Accident," *Selected Essays of G. K. Chesterton*, London: Collins, 1936, p. 68.
6. Wililiam James, *The Varieties of Religious Experience*, New York: The New American Library, a Mentor Book, 1958.

CHAPTER NINE

1. Clifford Geertz, *The Interpretation of Cultures*, New York: Basic Books, 1973, p. 90.
2. Edward Shils and Talcott Parsons, *Toward a General Theory of Action*, Cambridge: Harvard University Press, 1951.
3. Paul Ricoeur, *The Symbolism of Evil*, Boston: Beacon Press, 1967, pp. 232–278.
4. David Caplovitz, data cited in Andrew M. Greeley, *The Denominational Society*, Glenview, Ill: Scott, Foresman, 1972, p. 242.
5. John Kotre, *View From the Border*, Chicago: Aldine Publishing Co., 1971.
6. Andrew M. Greeley, *The Denominational Society*, p. 243.
7. William C. McCready, *Faith of Our Fathers: A Study of Religious Socialization*, Ph.D. dissertation, University of Illinois at Chicago, 1972 (University Microfilms).
8. William C. McCready and Nancy A. McCready, "Socialization and the Persistence of Religion," *Concilium*, 1 (1973).

CHAPTER TEN

1. Robert Wuthnow, "Recent Pattern of Secularization: A Problem of Generations?" *American Sociological Review*, (1976): 850–867.